Operations Management in China

Operations Management in China

Second Edition

Dr. Craig Seidelson

BUSINESS EXPERT PRESS
Leader in applied, concise business books

First published in 2022 by
Business Expert Press, LLC
222 East 46th Street, New York, NY 10017
www.businessexpertpress.com

ISBN-13: 978-1-95334-928-6 (paperback)
ISBN-13: 978-1-95334-929-3 (e-book)

Business Expert Press Supply and Operations Management Collection

Collection ISSN: 2156-8200 (print)
Collection ISSN: 2156-8189 (electronic)

Cover design by Charlene Kronstedt
Interior design by S4Carlisle Publishing Services Private Ltd., Chennai, India

First edition: 2020

10 9 8 7 6 5 4 3 2 1

Description

Leading business schools routinely offer undergraduate and postgraduate degrees in operations and supply chain management. Yet 200,000 U.S. jobs in supply chain management go unfilled each year owing to lack of talent. The talent that U.S. companies need, and that this book provides, is understanding how to make and buy products from China.

How important is China to U.S. operations? In 2018, U.S. imports from China reached $600 billion. Half of these imports were bought by U.S. manufacturers. A dependency on Chinese goods is even greater when looking at U.S. supply chains. Sixty cents of every dollar that U.S. consumers spend on goods made in China go to U.S. workers and companies.

Successful operations and supply chain managers understand manufacturing in China. This book takes readers inside Chinese organizations and shows how factories are built, labor is managed, goods are sourced, quality is controlled, and logistics are handled. Through this immersion experience, readers are able to see the opportunities and pitfalls in manufacturing in China.

Keywords

Chinese business; supply chain management; operations management; manufacturing in China

Contents

Preface

Authors use words to describe ideas. Wouldn't it be wonderful if by simply putting words on a page knowledge could be transferred? In reality, learning seldom works like this. To truly grasp ideas, readers need to be engaged.

Facts and figures are engaging, but there's only so much they can convey. To understand what's happening in China, readers need a more visceral connection. Throughout this book the author uses stories and photographs to make this connection.

It may be the case that how operations are described in the following pages isn't how they should be managed. It's up to readers to think critically about the material and form their own conclusions. This level of engagement promotes learning. But it can also be exhausting. That's why the author uses a very conversational tone in this book. That said, let's have a conversation about operations management in China.

Disclaimer

The author uses stories to help illustrate situations or concepts to readers. Stories are a combination of statements presented by third parties to the author and the author's experiences.

Stories were re-created from the author's memory, and thus no attempt was made to verify the accuracy of any third party statement. When presenting stories, the author has changed the names of persons, entities, and locations. Changes were made for creative purposes, inadvertently because of an inability to recall the circumstances with complete accuracy or simply to preserve the confidentiality of those involved.

No story necessarily relates to any current or former employers or represents policies adopted by them. In some instances, the stated conversations are modified or embellished or may have been wholly created and are thus fictitious. Likewise, no story is intended as a factual statement, description of an actual event, or a confirmation of any particular government, personal, or company policy. Although certain experiences underlying the stories may be factual, the stories themselves are fictionalized and intentionally changed to generically illustrate concepts and, as such, are merely a means to present concepts to readers in a different and interesting manner.

The author has also relied extensively on third party publications. Although cited works are consistent with the author's experiences, the author has not attempted to independently verify that any such publications or their contents are accurate or complete.

Furthermore, the author makes no claim that this work includes a complete treatment of any particular subject matter, including operations management or manufacturing in China. Similarly, the contents of this work are not intended as advice (legal or otherwise). The reader should not rely on this work as the sole source of information related to undertaking or preparing for work in China or otherwise.

Abbreviation

ACFTU	All-China Federation of Trade Union
AIC	Administration of Industry and Commerce
AQSIQ	General Administration of Quality Supervision, Inspection and Quarantine
ASTM	American Society for Testing and Materials
B2B	Business to Business
BIS	U.S. Bureau of Industry and Security
CAS	Chinese Academy of Sciences
CCC	China Compulsory Certificate
CCIC	China Certification and Inspection Group (CCIC)
CCP	Chinese Communist Party
CIB	China Commodity Inspection Bureau
CJV	Cooperative Joint Venture
CNAS	China National Accreditation Service
COGS	Cost of Goods Sold
CPA	Certified Public Accountant
CR	China Railway Corporation
DB	Provincial Standards
EAR	Export Regulations
EDB	Economic Development Bureau
EIA	Environmental Impact Assessment
EJV	Economic Joint Venture
EP	Environmental Protection
EPB	Environmental Protection Bureau
ETDZ	Economic and Technological Development Zone
FCL	Full Container Load
FDA	Food and Drug Administration
FDI	Foreign Direct Investment
FE	Fundamentals of Engineering
FIE	Foreign Invested Enterprise
FTL	Full Truckload Shipment
FTZ	Free Trade Zone

G20	The Group of Twenty countries accounting for approximately 80 percent of world trade
G7	Group of seven countries accounting for approximately 60 percent of global wealth
GB	Guobia
GDP	Gross Domestic Product
GM	General Manager
GW	Gigawatt
HIDZ	High-Tech Industrial Development Zone
HR	Human Resources
IP	Intellectual Property
ISO	International Standards Organization
IT	Information Technology
JV	Joint Venture
L/C	Letter of Credit
LCL	Less than Container Load
LLC	Limited Liability Corporation
MEP	Ministry of Environmental Protection
MFN	Most Favored Nation
MIC 2025	Made in China 2025
MNC	Multinational Corporation
MOF	Ministry of Finance
MOFCOM	Ministry of Commerce
MOLSS	Ministry of Labor and Social Security
MOR	Ministry of Rail
MOST	Ministry of Science and Technology
NDRC	National Development & Reform Commission
NEA	National Energy Administration
NEC	National Energy Commission
NEPA	National Environmental Protection Agency
NPC	National People's Congress
OECD	Organization for Economic Cooperation and Development
PO	Purchase Order
PPAP	Production Part Approval
PPI	Producer Price Index
PPP	Public Private Partnership
PRC	People's Republic of China
PSB	Public Security Bureau
PTE	Processing Trade Enterprise

Q	Enterprise Standards
R&D	Research and Development
RFQ	Request for Quote
RMB	Renminbi
RO	Representative Office
SAFE	State Administration of Foreign Exchange
SASAC	Assets Supervision and Administration Commission
SAT	State Administration of Taxation
SEZ	Special Economic Zone
SOE	State Owned Enterprise
TSB	Technical Supervision Bureau
VAT	Value Added Tax
WOFE	Wholly Owned Foreign Enterprise
WSB	Workers Safety Bureau
WTO	World Trade Organization

CHAPTER 1

Introduction

From 2000 through 2010, China's gross domestic product (GDP) averaged 10 percent growth year on year. This level of growth was eight times what the U.S. economy experienced over the same period.[1] Few sectors have felt the impact of China's emergence more than U.S. manufacturing.

> *"Can you believe the prices on these parts from China?"*
>
> *"I guess we'll just have to step up our Lean Manufacturing efforts."*
>
> *"Are you kidding? These prices are lower than our material costs. There's no way to close this kind of gap with efficiency improvements."*
>
> *"What are you suggesting? We can't just exit the business."*
>
> *"I know. But we can't compete with these prices."*
>
> *"Our quality is better."*
>
> *"Sure. But, only if people are willing to pay for it."*

The United States imports more goods from China than from any other country. In 2018, U.S. imports from China reached approximately $600 billion, or almost a quarter of all imports.[2] In spite of these statistics, Sara Bongiorni and her family embarked on the seemingly impossible. They attempted to live a year without buying anything made in China. Recounting their experiences in *A Year Without "Made in China": One*

---

[1] *US Bureau of Economic Analysis.* 2019. "US GDP Growth Rate by Year," www.multpl.com/us-gdp-growth-rate/table/by-year, (accessed December 9, 2019).

[2] D. Kopf. 2019. "The US Will Have a Hard Time Not Getting These Products from China," *Quartz.* https://qz.com/1654798/these-are-the-products-the-us-is-most-reliant-on-china-for/, (accessed July 3, 2019).

Family's True Life Adventure in the Global Economy, she noted, "There's just really no way to live what would be considered an ordinary consumer life without a heavy reliance on merchandise from China."[3]

The difficulties Sara and her family faced over a decade ago would be much greater today. As Figure 1.1 shows, China has been the worldwide leader in manufacturing since 2010.[4]

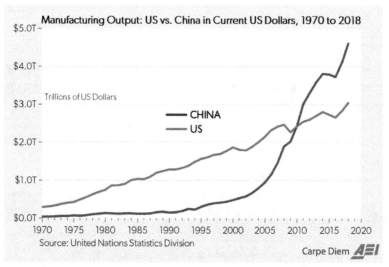

Figure 1.1 China has surpassed the United States in manufacturing output

Source: Courtesy of Mark Perry

To be fair, there are better measures of manufacturing strength than goods produced. Value added levels the playing field by discounting sales for imports and cost of materials and inventory. That said, China's $3-trillion value added is still the world's largest. And the United States is still a distant second, with a 40 percent lower value add than China.[5]

---

[3]*Foreign Policy.* 2007. "Seven Questions: Can You Live without China?" http://foreignpolicy.com/2007/07/11/seven-questions-can-you-live-without-china/, (accessed November 17, 2018).

[4]W. Hunter. 2012. "China Beating BRA in Manufacturing," *Occidental Dissent.* www.occidentaldissent.com/2012/12/15/china-beating-bra-in-manufacturing/, (accessed September 9, 2016).

[5]M. Levinson. 2018. "US Manufacturing in International Perspective," *Congressional Research Service.* https://fas.org/sgp/crs/misc/R42135.pdf, (accessed December 15, 2019).

Who's buying all these made-in-China products? Most are consumed in China. Of the remainder, the single largest amount (e.g., 18 percent in 2018) ends up in the United States.[6]

Against the flood of low-cost Chinese imports, how have U.S. manufactures fared? Not very well. From 2001 through 2015, U.S. companies closed 40,000 factories and sent one out of every 10 manufacturing jobs to China.[7]

Can the remaining U.S. manufacturers compete? It wouldn't appear so. By 2017 the U.S. trade deficit with China hit a record $375 billion. China now accounts for roughly 70 percent of the total U.S. trade deficit.[8] The need to update trade policy with China has been described as "it is not a question of meeting halfway, it is a question of rebalancing the asymmetry and a question of openness."[9]

In response to the trade imbalance, the U.S. government imposed a 25 percent tariff on $34 billion worth of Chinese imports in July 2018. The Chinese government responded with an identical tariff on the same amount of U.S. imports.[10] A month later, both sides extended their tariffs to include an additional $50 billion worth of imports. By mid-2020, the U.S. had imposed four rounds of tariffs on more than $360 billion worth of Chinese goods. Chinese tariffs on U.S. goods totaled more than $110 billion.

Both sides have felt the impact of the trade war. China is experiencing its slowest GDP growth in almost 30 years. U.S. manufacturing growth

---

[6]K. Amadeo. 2020. "China's Economy and Its Effect on the U.S. Economy," *World Economy: Asia.* https://www.thebalance.com/china-economy-facts-effect-on-us-economy-3306345, (accessed June 2, 2020).

[7]R. Scott. 2012. "The China Toll," *Economic Policy Institute.* www.epi.org/publication/bp345-china-growing-trade-deficit-cost/, (accessed June 17, 2016).

[8]J. Schlesinger and H. Torry. 2018. "U.S. Trade Deficit Grew to $566 Billion in 2017, Its Widest Mark in Nine Years," *The Wall Street Journal.* www.wsj.com/articles/u-s-trade-gap-highest-in-nine-years-in-december-1517923918, (accessed July 16, 2019).

[9]Lau, S. 2020. "China Pledges Expanded Trade with EU But Stops Short on Market Access Concessions," *South China Morning Post.* https://www.scmp.com/news/china/diplomacy/article/3101552/china-pledges-expanded-trade-eu-stops-short-market-access, (accessed September 15, 2020).

[10]M. Bomey. 2018. "How President Trump's Chinese Tariffs Affect American Consumers," *USA Today.* www.usatoday.com/story/money/2018/07/06/president-trumps-china-tariffs-consumer-impact/762982002/, (accessed September 15, 2019).

is at its lowest level in over 10 years. In response to the economic crisis, President Trump and China's Vice Premier Liu He signed the U.S.–China Phase One trade deal. At the heart of the agreement was a promise to increase Chinese imports from the United States by $200 billion by 2022. About 40 percent of this increase is to be in manufactured goods. Beijing also promises to improve foreign access to its financial markets and discontinue use of competitive currency devaluation. In exchange, the United States promised to halve its tariff rate on $120 billion worth of Chinese goods.

Enter COVID-19. The World Bank estimates that the viral pandemic will ultimately shrink the global economy by 5.2 percent.[11] The United States and Chinese economies have been particularly hard hit by the virus. In the first half of 2020, the United States recorded over 50 million job losses and a 5 percent drop in GDP. The mainland Chinese economy contracted roughly 7 percent. In light of economic slowdowns on both sides, follow-through on the U.S.– China trade deal is far from guaranteed. For example, by 2022, China agreed to increase U.S. agricultural imports by $32 billion compared with 2017 levels. Yet, as of mid-2020, Chinese imports were tracking at less than half the level needed to reach agreed targets.

Conventional wisdom says that "tariffs make supply chains more costly, forcing companies to operate at a loss [until] the conflict is resolved."[12] Unfortunately, even with a Phase One trade deal in place, conflict between the United States and China is far from being resolved. In 2020 alone:

---

[11]The World Bank. 2020. "COVID-19 to Plunge Global Economy into Worst Recession since World War II," https://www.worldbank.org/en/news/press-release/2020/06/08/covid-19-to-plunge-global-economy-into-worst-recession-since-world-war-ii, (accessed August 8, 2020).

[12]M. Sheetz. 2018. "Here's Where We Are in the Trade War—And What It Means," *CNBC—Markets*. https://www.cfr.org/blog/us-dependence-pharmaceutical-productschina#:~:text=In%20the%20discussion%2C%20Gary%20Cohn,United%20States%20came%20from%20China., (accessed October 12, 2018).

- U.S. Secretary of State Pompeo described long-standing Chinese claims in the South China Sea as "completely unlawful."[13] The Trump administration subsequently placed 24 Chinese companies allegedly involved in helping to construct artificial islands in region on an Entities List.
- The U.S. Department of Commerce, Bureau of Industry and Security (BIS) placed more than 300 Chinese companies on its Entities List. The List identifies persons and/or organizations "that the U.S. government has identified as acting contrary to U.S. national security or foreign policy interests."[14] Conducting business with companies on the list requires difficult to attain licenses through Export Administration Regulations.
- In response to a series of perceived pro-Taiwan bills introduced in the U.S. Congress, China's Foreign Ministry "firmly opposes any official interactions between the U.S. and Taiwan and has made stern representations with the U.S. side over this issue."[15]
- The Trump administration alleged China's largest technology company, Huawei, was a front for the Communist Party. The U.S. Commerce Department responded with sanctions that "restrict any foreign semiconductor company from selling chips developed

---

[13]M. Pompeo. 2020. "U.S. Position on Maritime Claims in the South China Sea," U.S. Dept. of State Press Statement. https://www.state.gov/u-s-position-on-maritime-claims-in-the-south-china-sea/#:~:text=We%20are%20making%20clear%3A%20Beijing's,of%20bullying%20to%20control%20them.&text=Beijing%20has%20offered%20no%20coherent,formally%20announcing%20it%20in%202009, (accessed August 8, 2020).

[14]*Reed Smith*. 2020. "U.S. Department of Commerce designates 33 Chinese companies on the Entity List and Issues Related Supply Chain Business Advisory," https://www.reedsmith.com/en/perspectives/2020/07/us-department-of-commerce-designates-33-chinese-companies, (accessed Sept. 1, 2020).

[15]R. Jennings. 2020. "Why US Lawmakers Introduce Bill After Bill to Help Taiwan," *Voice of America*. https://www.voanews.com/east-asia-pacific/why-us-lawmakers-introduce-bill-after-bill-help-taiwan, (accessed August 11, 2020).

or produced using US software or technology to Huawei, without first obtaining a license."[16]

- Hong Kong's preferential trading status with the United States ended after Beijing imposed a new nation security law on the autonomous region. According to Amnesty International, the law's 66 articles "can easily become catch-all offences used in politically motivated prosecutions with potentially heavy penalties."[17]

- President Trump issued an executive order attempting to ban Chinese social media apps TikTok and WeChat on the grounds that American's personal information could be provided to Chinese authorities.

- Accusations of intellectual property theft prompted the U.S. government to order closure of China's consulate in Houston, Texas. The Chinese government responded by ordering the closure of the U.S. consulate in Chengdu, China.

- Thousands of Chinese graduate students and researchers lost their U.S. visas owing to suspected ties with the Chinese People's Liberation Army.

- Under new U.S. Federal Registry dual use rules, export licenses are now required for "U.S. companies to sell certain items to companies in China that support the military, even if the products are for civilian use."[18]

- China's Ministry of Commerce (MOFCOM) and the Ministry of Science and Technology added 23 technologies to the list of restricted exports requiring a license to transfers. These technologies include drone technology, ultra-high voltage transmission, clean coal power generation, and quantum encryption.

---

[16]Pham, S. 2020. "New Sanctions Deal 'Lethal Blow' to Huawei. China Decries US Bullying," *CNN Business*. https://www.cnn.com/2020/08/17/tech/huawei-us-sanctions-hnk-intl/index.html, (accessed Sept. 1, 2020).

[17]*Amnesty International*. 2020. "Hong Kong's National Security Law: 10 Things You Should Know," https://www.amnesty.org/en/latest/news/2020/07/hong-kong-national-security-law-10-things-you-need-to-know/, (accessed Sept. 1, 2020).

[18]K. Friefeld. 2020. "U.S. Imposes New Rules on Exports to China to Keep Them from Its Military," *Reuters*. https://www.reuters.com/article/us-usa-china-exports/us-imposes-new-rules-on-exports-to-china-to-keep-them-from-its-military-idUSKCN2291SR, (accessed September 2, 2020).

- Under the *Rules on Counteracting Unjustified Extraterritorial Application of Foreign Legislation and Other Measures,* MOFCOM prohibited firms from complying with foreign laws banning transactions with Chinese companies and individuals.

Amid the economic and sociopolitical turmoil, President Joe Biden signed the "Made in America" executive order limiting how much federal agencies can spend on foreign products and how much foreign content is permissible in government contracts. Likewise, Biden's head of the Commerce Department spoke specifically about the need for "aggressive trade enforcement actions to combat unfair trade practices from China and other nations that undercut American manufacturing."[19] China responded with a newly created Beijing Financial Court responsible for hearing lawsuits brought against overseas financial entities accused of damaging Chinese business interests.

To mitigate policy-driven disruptions in their supply chains, more and more U.S. companies are implementing a "China Plus One" strategy. For example, a 2020 PricewaterhouseCoopers survey of U.S. chief financial officers (CFOs) found 51 percent of respondents identified "developing alternate options for sourcing" as their top supply chain strategy.[20] Yet it's highly unlikely U.S. companies will decouple their links with China, considering $0.60 of every dollar U.S. consumers spend on goods made in China go to U.S. workers and companies.[21] The fact is that at every level of their supply chains U.S. companies will continue to need managers

---

[19]D. Shepardson. 2021. "Biden's Commerce Pick Pledges Aggressive Enforcement to Combat 'Unfair' Chinese Trade Practices," *Reuters.* https://finance.yahoo.com/news/bidens-commerce-pick-pledges-aggressive-100000975.html, (accessed January 27, 2021).
[20]A. Van Dam. 2019. "Made in China: Most of What You Pay Goes to U.S. Workers and Businesses, Despite What the Label Says," *The Washington Post.* www.washingtonpost.com/business/2019/01/11/reminder-most-what-you-pay-made-china-product-goes-us-workers-businesses/, (accessed January 5, 2020).
[21]T. Shortell, J. Hills., and L. Hung. 2020. "Refocusing Supply Chains in the COVID-19 Era," *CBRE.* http://cbre.vo.llnwd.net/grgservices/secure/Asia%20Pacific%20ViewPoint_Refocusing%20Supply%20Chains%20in%20the%20COVID-19%20Era.pdf?e=1596815683&h=c15077e27efde40ac0e0a5decd1c55e7, (accessed August 7, 2020).

who understand how to work and compete with Chinese operations. In this book, readers will learn how:

- Foreign investments are made in China
- Facilities are built
- Labor is managed
- Procurement is handled
- Quality is maintained
- And goods are transported

With a firm grasp of how things *should* work in China, readers will also see how they *don't* work, namely,

- Nearly all business activities are regulated
- Many employees are quitting
- Conflicts of interest abound
- Quality's low
- Productivity's lower
- Getting anything from point A to point B can be riddled with inefficiencies.

CHAPTER 2

Factory Investment

How badly do U.S. companies need a manufacturing presence in China? On the surface, it doesn't appear as if U.S. consumers spend all that much on Chinese-made products. In 2017, trade with China averaged only 3 percent of U.S. gross domestic product (GDP). In 11 states, according to Figure 2.1, the amount spent on Chinese goods was less than 1.5 percent of GDP.

Figure 2.1 U.S. trade with China as a percentage of GDP by state, 2017

These percentages, however, are misleading. Almost two-thirds of all U.S. spending is on domestic services such as housing, insurance, pensions, health care, and education.[1] When seen in terms of only what U.S. consumers spend on durable goods, Chinese-made products account for $0.12 of every $1.[2]

In theory, demand for Chinese imports over U.S. exports should produce an upward pressure on China's currency (RMB). The trade imbalance should likewise produce a downward pressure on the U.S. dollar. As the dollar becomes weaker, U.S.-made goods become more cost competitive. The trade imbalance should be self-correcting.

Unfortunately, this isn't the case when trading with China. As the RMB becomes stronger, the Chinese government prints more of it. With more RMB notes in circulation, the currency remains weak. A weak RMB keeps the prices of Chinese-made goods low, which, in turn, keeps exports high. The U.S. government hasn't complained too loudly because China is the second largest foreign holder of U.S. Treasury bills.[3]

How undervalued is the RMB? From 2001 through 2005, China's GDP rose 250 percent. At the same time, employment rose a mere 12 percent and inflation remained below 6 percent. If government figures are correct, the RMB was at least 40 percent undervalued in 2007.[4] By 2019, following multiple currency appreciations and devaluations by the People's Bank of China, the RMB was 25 percent undervalued.[5]

---

[1] K. Amedeo. 2020. "Consumer Spending Statistics and Current Trends," *The Balance*. www.thebalance.com/consumer-spending-trends-and-current-statistics-3305916, (accessed February 6, 2020).

[2] G. Hale and B. Hobijn. 2011. "The US Content of 'Made in China,'" *Federal Reserve of San Francisco Economic Letter*. www.frbsf.org/economic-research/publications/economic-letter/2011/august/us-made-in-china/, (accessed August 9, 2018).

[3] K. Amadeo. 2020. "China's Economy and Its Effect on the U.S. Economy," *The Balance*. www.thebalance.com/china-economy-facts-effect-on-us-economy-3306345, (accessed February 6, 2020).

[4] *CRSReport.com*. 2008. "China's Currency: Economic Issues and Options for U.S. Trade Policy," www.everycrsreport.com/reports/RL32165.html, (accessed June 23, 2018).

[5] *Investopedia*. 2019. "The Impact of China Devaluating the Yuan," www.investopedia.com/trading/chinese-devaluation-yuan/, (accessed January 5, 2020).

Faced with a persistently weak RMB and a 1,000 percent increase in imports since China joined the World Trade Organization (WTO) in 2001, U.S. manufacturers have dramatically downsized operations.[6] From 2001 to 2015, U.S. companies cut nearly 3.5 million jobs.[7] Almost 80 percent of these jobs were in manufacturing. And nearly half of those went to China.[8] In an attempt to stem the flow of Chinese products into and jobs out of the United States, the Trump administration began implementing tariffs on Chinese goods in 2018. By 2020, the United States was taxing more than $360 billion worth of Chinese imports. The Chinese responded with tariffs on more than $110 billion worth of U.S. imports and asked for a WTO investigation. After 2 years of deliberation, the WTO concluded that the U.S. had not justified the additional duties and that any bilateral deals negotiated outside of the WTO couldn't be considered a settlement. The U.S. trade representative responded that "the ruling was evidence of the WTO's ineffectiveness."[9]

In light of the ongoing U.S.–China trade war, a fundamental question remains: "Can made-in-USA compete with made-in-China?" As Table 2.1 shows, it depends largely on what's being made.

Four product categories (electronics, machinery, clothing, and plastics) account for roughly 50 percent of all Chinese exports.[10] Figure 2.2 shows that U.S. states where these products are traditionally manufactured have lost between 2 and 4 percent of employment to China.

---

[6]*Office of the United States Trade Representative.* 2019. "The People's Republic of China: US-China Trade Facts," https://ustr.gov/countries-regions/china-mongolia-taiwan/peoples-republic-china, (accessed January 30, 2020).

[7]R. Scott. 2017. "Growth in U.S.–China Trade Deficit between 2001 and 2015 Cost 3.4 Million Jobs," *Economic Policy Institute.* www.epi.org/publication/growth-in-u-s-china-trade-deficit-between-2001-and-2015-cost-3-4-million-jobs-heres-how-to-rebalance-trade-and-rebuild-american-manufacturing/, (accessed May 6, 2018).

[8]R. Scott. 2012. "The China Toll," *Economic Policy Institute.* www.epi.org/publication/bp345-china-growing-trade-deficit-cost/, (accessed August 29, 2018).

[9]Klien, J. 2020. "WTO Says Donald Trump's Tariffs on Chinese Goods Violate Global Trade Rules," *South China Morning Post.* https://amp-scmp-com.cdn.ampproject.org/c/s/amp.scmp.com/news/world/united-states-canada/article/3101681/wto-rules-against-trumps-tariffs-china, (accessed September 17, 2020).

[10]D. Workmann. 2020. "China's Top 10 Exports," *World's Top Exports.* www.worldstopexports.com/chinas-top-10-exports/1952, (accessed March 17, 2018).

Table 2.1 Percentages of products made in China

Artificial Christmas lights	85%
Shoes	72%
Umbrellas	70%
Buttons	60%
Kitchen appliances	50%
Toys	50%
U.S. imports that go to Walmart	9%

Statistic Brain Research Institute, 2018, www.statisticbrain.com/china-manufacturing-statistics/

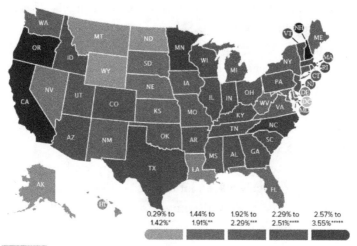

* 10 least-affected states, plus D.C.
** 10 next-least-affected states
*** 10 middle affected states
**** 10 next-most-affected states
***** 10 most-affected states

Source: Authors' analysis of U.S. Census Bureau 2013, U.S. International Trade Commission 2018, and Bureau of Labor Statistics Employment Projections program 2017a and 2017b. For a more detailed explanation of data sources and computations, see the appendix.

Economic Policy Institute

Figure 2.2 Net U.S. jobs displaced owing to the goods trade deficit with China as a share of total state employment, 2001 to 2017

Source: Reprinted from "The China Toll Deepens" by R. Scott and Z. Mokhiber. 2018, Retrieved from www.epi.org.

U.S. computer and electronics companies have been hit particularly hard by Chinese imports. From 2000 through 2011, they cut nearly 1,000,000 jobs. Over the same period, U.S. apparel companies lost 200,000 jobs. Metal workers and furniture makers didn't fare much better. Each lost over 100,000 jobs.[11]

As jobs left the United States, companies set up operations in China. Today, of the approximately 1 million multinational corporations (MNCs) around the world, one-third have operations in China. Among Fortune 500 companies, the percentage is even greater: Roughly 80 percent have operations in China. To put foreign investment in perspective, as of 2018, China was home to approximately 36,000 foreign-invested enterprises (FIEs).[12] U.S.-invested operations led the way, with plants numbering in the tens of thousands (Figure 2.3).

U.S. Manufacturing Plants, China, 2008

Courtesy: Robert South

Figure 2.3 U.S.-invested manufacturing plants in China

Source: Adapted from "How U.S. Companies Decide Where to Locate Their Chinese Factories," by J. Zimmerman, 2008, Reprinted with permission by Changjoo Kim.

[11]R. Scott. 2012. "The China toll," *Economic Policy Institute*. www.epi.org/publication/bp345-china-growing-trade-deficit-cost/, (accessed August 29, 2018).

[12]J. Zimmerman. 2012. "How U.S. Companies Decide Where to Locate Their Chinese Factories," *CityLab*. www.citylab.com/life/2012/03/how-us-companies-decide-where-build-their-chinese-factories/1412/, (accessed November 16, 2017).

In recent years, the United States–China trade war coupled with the COVID-19 pandemic and increased cost of manufacturing in China has produced a downward pressure on foreign direct investment (FDI) into China. For example, in the first 6 months of 2020 "total capital deployed through direct and venture capital investments fell to an estimated $10.9 billion, from $26 billion at its 2016 peak."[13] Still, U.S.-invested operations export approximately $100 billion worth of Chinese-made products back to the United States every year. Their exports alone account for 20 percent of all U.S. imports from China. U.S.-invested operations in China aren't the only ones targeting U.S. consumers. Close to 50 percent of all U.S. imports come from FIEs in China.[14] MNC companies clearly rely on their Chinese operations to boost sales. But what about profits? FIEs accounted for roughly a quarter of China's industrial profits in 2010, while employing only 10 percent of labor.[15]

With so many foreign companies setting up profitable operations in China, how hard can it be? In a word, *very*. Nothing happens in an FIE without government involvement. One reason why is the sheer size and scope of the Chinese government. Heading the 10 million or so civil servants inside the one-party system is a president (also known as party secretary). The president (with the approval of the 2,980 delegates to the National People's Congress) appoints a premier. The premier heads a state council, which includes an executive vice premier, three vice premiers, five state councilors, and 25 ministers. This central government, in addition to managing 21 ministries, the central bank, and three commissions, oversees heads of 23 provinces, four municipalities (Beijing, Tianjin,

[13] *The New India Express.* 2020. "Foreign Companies Shifting Production Out of China a 'Normal Market Phenomenon': Chinese Official," https://www.newindianexpress.com/world/2020/sep/17/foreign-companies-shifting-production-out-of-china-a-normal-market-phenomenon-chinese-official-2198211.html, (accessed September 20, 2020).

[14] R. Hoffmann. 2014. "Emerging Multinational Companies in China," *Ecovis.* www.ecovis.com/focus-china/emerging-multinational-companies-china-12/, (accessed June 19, 2017).

[15] *The World Bank.* 2010. "Foreign Direct Investment: The China Story," www.worldbank.org/en/news/feature/2010/07/16/foreign-direct-investment-china-story, (accessed July 20, 2018).

Shanghai, Chongqing), five autonomous regions (Guangxi, Inner Mongolia, Tibet, Ningxia, Xinjiang), and two special administrative regions (Hong Kong, Macau). Subsequent levels of government include prefectures, counties, districts, cities, and towns. Each higher administrative level in the chain supervises the level immediately beneath it. Supervision entails having the power to change or annul any decisions seen as inappropriate.

The state council entrusts the National Development and Reform Commission (NDRC)[16] with collecting input from the ministries to write the country's economic goals for each upcoming 5 years. In the 13th Plan (2015 through 2020), the NDRC introduced "doing away with foreign investment rules and governing all legally-established companies in China under the same laws and regulations."[17] That didn't happen. As of 2020, Chinese rules for foreign investment remain the most restrictive of those of all countries in the G20.[18] Currently, the NDRC and MOC are responsible for security reviews of all controlling foreign investment in the areas of energy, natural resources, agriculture, internet technology, and financial services. The chief economist at a globally renowned investment strategy group commented: "If you are running a business in developed markets, you know how to price in your costs. But in China, it is impossible to price in the regulatory risk."[19]

The Ministry of Commerce (MOFCOM) oversees China's foreign investment rules. One way it does this is by publishing a *Catalog for the Guidance of Foreign Invested Enterprises*. As of 2015, the Catalog contained

---

[16]The NDRC was formally known as the State Planning Commission.

[17]*China Business Review.* 2016. "13th Five Year Plan Stresses Economic Restructuring," www.chinabusinessreview.com/13th-five-year-plan-stresses-economic-restructuring/, (accessed February 20, 2018).

[18]*US Chamber of Commerce.* 2017. "Made in China 2025: Global Ambitions Built on Local Protections," www.uschamber.com/report/made-china-2025-global-ambitions-built-local-protections-0, (accessed July 18, 2018).

[19]Yeung, K. 2021. "China's State-Led Economy Makes It Clear for Foreign Firms: You're Either OK with Regulatory Requirements, Or You're Out," *South China Morning Post.* https://www.scmp.com/economy/china-economy/article/3119782/chinas-state-led-economy-makes-it-clear-foreign-firms-youre, (accessed February 2, 2021).

over 1,000 regulations. Complying with so many regulations is only part of the challenge for operations managers. The other is keeping track of changes. The Catalog has been revised five times since 1995.

As of 2020, foreign investment is still classified as "prohibited," "restricted," or "encouraged." The prohibited sector is off limits to foreign investment.[20] Foreigners can, however, invest in restricted sectors. As of 2015, there were 40 restricted sectors. These include automobile manufacturing, civil aviation, education, banking, investment, insurance, petroleum, railway equipment, and telecommunications. Foreign investment in these sectors comes with a number of restrictions. For example, as of 2019, foreigners are restricted to joint ventures (JVs) in which Chinese partners hold a majority interest. In addition, Chinese nationals in these organizations must perform certain key functions such as auditing and accounting. The U.S. Chamber of Commerce has equated such JV restrictions to de facto technology transfer requirements to enter the Chinese market.[21] In an effort to ease trade friction, foreign vehicle manufacturers, as of 2020, are permitted to own more than 50 percent of their JVs with Chinese electric car companies. By 2022, it is reported, foreign equity restrictions will be lifted on gasoline-powered vehicles.[22]

In light of these difficulties, most foreign-invested operations in China are in "encouraged" sectors. Unfortunately, knowing whether an investment is encouraged or restricted isn't always easy. Encouraged activities can be simultaneously listed as restricted. Examples include the design, manufacture, and repair of airplanes. These encouraged businesses are still restricted to JVs in which Chinese partners hold a majority interest.[23]

---

[20]Prohibited sectors are typically energy intensive, heavily polluting, or involved in extracting natural resources.

[21]*US Chamber of Commerce.* 2017. "Made in China 2025: Global Ambitions Built on Local Protections," www.uschamber.com/report/made-china-2025-global-ambitions-built-local-protections-0, (accessed July 18, 2018).

[22]*Autovista Group.* 2018. "China to Drop 50:50 Rule and Allow Foreign Majorities in Joint Ventures," https://autovistagroup.com/news-and-insights/china-drop-5050-rule-and-allow-foreign-majorities-joint-ventures, (accessed February 19, 2019).

[23]A. Koty and Z. Qian. 2017. *China Briefing.* www.china-briefing.com/news/2017/07/11/china-releases-2017-foreign-investment-catalogue-opening-access-new-industries.html, (accessed August 20, 2019).

Even though national commissions and ministries make China's FDI rules, approvals and enforcement happen at the provincial, municipal, or township levels. This approach can be described as "achieving national goals using local methods." In other words, during times of reform, local authorities have traditionally been given a fairly wide latitude in interpreting what can and can't be done. Since President Xi Jinping assumed power in 2012, there's been a gradual shift away from the "local methods" model. An obvious benefit for foreign investors is improved standardization of business rules and practices. The problem is that "strict adherence to Party orders has stifled decentralized initiative at lower levels of government [creating] outright paralysis in local administrative action and policy implementation."[24]

Recent changes notwithstanding, few agencies in China hold as much sway over operations management as the local Economic Development Bureau (EDB). The EDB writes local economic regulations, zones property, and approves all investment. When passing judgment on investment, local EDB officials have typically asked for very detailed plans. Plans have traditionally covered areas such as proposed business activities, location, factory layout, start-up capitalization, debt, and organizational structure.

In their proposals, foreign investors must choose one of four paths.[25]

- A representative office (RO)
- An equity joint venture (EJV)
- A cooperative joint venture (CJV)
- Or a wholly owned foreign enterprise (WOFE)

New investors to China might be tempted to set up an RO. It's the easiest and least expensive. In less than a month an RO can be up and running as long as three conditions are met:

1. A lease agreement is signed for at least a year.

---

[24]S. Heilmann. 2016. "Leninism Upgraded: Xi Jiping's Authoritarian Innovations," *China Economic Quarterly*. www.merics.org/sites/default/files/201803/Heilmann_Leninism_Upgraded_China_Economic_Quarterly_Dec.2016.pdf, (accessed August 20, 2018).

[25]As part of restructuring efforts, the State Council has allowed some foreign companies to form JVs with state-owned enterprises (SOEs).

2. A chief representative manages day-to-day activities.
3. The RO is owned by a foreign corporation or limited liability company (LLC).

Unfortunately, ROs have many limitations, some of which are as follows[26]:

- They can't earn income.
- They can't bill customers, sign contracts, or charge fees.
- Taxes are assessed on gross expenses.

Unable to perform even the most basic business functions with an RO, investors might choose another path. One of those options is a JV.[27] In 2014, China's 6,400 JVs accounted for 19 percent of all FDI.[28]

Compared with ROs, JVs require a lot more time and money to set up. There are prospective partners to meet, local officials to consult with, and paperwork to fill out. All of this can take over a year to complete. In the end, all parties (including local officials) need to agree on what the JV will do (as described in its business license) and how it will be organized (as described in its articles of incorporation).

The importance of JV articles cannot be overstated. A good set of articles will address the following:

- Who's investing?
- What's being invested?
- By when will investments be made?
- Who sits on the board of directors?

---

[26]S. O'Regan. 2015. "Tax Benefits of Changing from an RO to a WFOE," *China Briefing*. www.china-briefing.com/news/2015/03/26/tax-benefits-of-changing-from-an-ro-to-a-wfoe.html, (accessed August 16, 2018).

[27]ROs, JVs, and WOFEs are all distinct business types. It isn't possible to simply switch from one to another. The application process must be restarted.

[28]N. Lang, et al. 2016. "How to Successfully Manage Joint Ventures in China," *Boston Consulting Group*. www.bcg.com/publications/2016/corporate-development-finance-how-to-successfully-manage-joint-ventures-in-china.aspx, (accessed August 19, 2019).

- What are their roles and responsibilities?
- How will profits be distributed?

The Chinese partner will typically want to manage day-to-day operations. The Chinese partner will usually ask the foreign partner to contribute some combination of capital, technology, and access to export markets. In exchange, the foreign partner will typically ask the Chinese partner to provide production facilities, trained workers, an established supply chain, and domestic customers.

What are local government officials expecting from foreign-invested JVs? Assurances that the operation will bring in technology, hire a lot of people, and have enough seed money to cover expenses until profits can sustain operations. Government involvement in operations doesn't end once local officials and investors agree on articles. A number of government certificates are needed.

- The State Administration of Industry and Commerce (AIC) must issue name approval and a business license.
- MOFCOM must issue a certificate of business.
- The public security bureau (PSB) must issue a company seal.
- The technical supervision bureau (TSB) must issue an organization code.
- The tax bureau must issue a tax certificate.
- The state administration of foreign exchange (SAFE) must approve the company's foreign currency trading account.

With government-issued documents in hand, it's time for operations managers to start delivering on promises made in articles of incorporation. In the case of EJVs, the promise is for equity investment. Traditionally, foreign equity has come with a number of strings attached.

- Foreign equipment, cash, materials, and intellectual property count toward equity investment.
- Foreign labor doesn't count toward investment.

- China-based equipment, cash, materials, land, or intellectual property (even if purchased by the foreign party) doesn't count toward investment.

What counts and doesn't count toward foreign capital contribution is further complicated by the fact that Chinese auditing standards do not always align with international standards. It wouldn't be unusual for auditors to find:

- Local balance sheets are overstating the value of outdated or poorly maintained equipment.
- Mandatory contributions toward social welfare benefits, pensions, maternity leave, housing benefits, unemployment, or disability have gone unpaid for years.
- Account receivables with little prospect of ever being collected are booked as assets.

[An engineer was trying to find a replacement pulley for a machine. The pulley looked like nothing he'd ever seen before.]
"Mr. Zhang, what kind of pulley is this?"
"It's off a drive motor."
"Why's it shaped like a cone?"
"To slow the machine down, the operator slips the drive belt off a large-diameter track and puts it on a smaller one."
"But this machine was built in 2002. Surely, Chinese machines used electric drives to control speed in 2002."
"Yes. But this machine was based on one built in 1970."

The valuation of imported equipment isn't necessarily based on market or depreciable value but on inspection reports put together by China Certification and Inspection Group (CCIC) associates located in the asset's country of origin. The CCIC inspector's first job is to determine whether a prospective import is prohibited, restricted, or transferable under China's *Regulations on the Import and Export of Technology*. Prohibited technologies can't be imported. Transferable technologies can be imported. Restricted technologies fall somewhere in the middle; they can be imported but only with government approval.[29] Generally speaking, approval isn't given for old or used equipment. Assuming technology can be imported, the CCIC inspector's next job is to assess condition and value. The China Tax Bureau uses this valuation to assign any relevant duties or value added tax (VAT).[30]

Foreign engineers spent over a year designing a low-cost manufacturing process for the China JV. To keep cost down, standard U.S. machines would be imported and upgraded in China.

Very few Chinese equipment manufactures were interested in modifying imported machines. Of the few quotes received, prices were nearly the same as buying new Chinese machines.

No one at company headquarters knew much about Chinese machines. Yet modifications had been successfully tested. And all necessary parts were readily available in China. The foreign project manager decided to stick with the plan and modify imported machines in China.

Problems appeared almost immediately. Regardless of drawings provided or instructions given to the builder, technicians did things their own way.

As the delivery date approached, it was clear that machine modifications were behind schedule. Days late turned into weeks, and weeks into months. Eventually, the machine builder asked for help.

The project manager sent a team of foreign engineers and technicians to China. They spent the next 2 months finishing modifications with the builder.

When it came time to install equipment, the local finance manager shared how pleased he was with the project manager.

"Considering how much we've spent on tooling, I was worried the machines would never run."

"Chinese tooling isn't that expensive."

---

[29]Investors intending to import U.S. equipment must determine whether U.S. export is subject to U.S. Bureau of Industry and Security (BIS) regulations (EAR). If regulations exist, a U.S. export license is needed prior to shipping.

[30]VAT rebates on imported equipment are no longer common.

> *"We're not using Chinese tooling."*
>
> *"But local tooling was a big part of our cost savings. I never approved imported tooling."*
>
> *"You were busy working on machine issues. I approved the purchase orders."*
>
> *"Why?"*
>
> *"To meet the foreign equity contribution."*
>
> *"That doesn't make sense. We've already overspent the machine modification budget. Why would we need to spend additional money importing tooling?"*
>
> *"As the foreign partner, you spent money. But it wasn't foreign money. Modifications occurred in China, so none of that expenditure counted toward the equity contribution."*
>
> *"So you're saying we didn't save any money doing machine modifications in China?"*
>
> *"Sure we did. It allowed us to buy imported tooling."*

In the past, statutes defined minimum foreign investment by industry. Statutes also defined when investments needed to be made. For example,

- 15 percent of all foreign equity needed to be contributed within 90 days of local government approval. The remainder needed to be invested within 2 years.
- Foreign equity couldn't be less than 25 percent of a venture's total value.
- If debt plus equity was less than US$3 million, foreign equity needed to cover at least 70 percent of total investment.
- If debt plus equity was more than $3 million (but less than $10 million), foreign equity needed to cover at least half of total investment.

Following the global recession (2007 through 2009), most foreign investment requirements have been dropped. By 2016, the Standing Committee of the National People's Congress revised *Wholly Foreign Owned Enterprises Law, Sino-Foreign Equity Joint Ventures Law,* and *Sino-Foreign*

Cooperative Joint Venture Law.[31] In theory, FIEs operating in encouraged industries are no longer examined by government authorities. They need only file their intentions with the government. In practice, company articles still specify how much will be invested and when investments will be made. Since articles must be submitted to the local AIC, it can be the case that local officials are less inclined to process, much less subsidize, ventures they perceive as underfunded.

One way around valuation issues is setting up CJVs. In CJVs, profit sharing isn't necessarily tied to each partner's equity contribution. And foreign contributions that don't count toward equity in EJVs can be considered in CJVs. The problem with CJVs is everything's open to interpretation and negotiation. As a result, EJVs outnumber CJVs nearly 20 to 1.

Whichever JV path is chosen, if the venture is classified as "encouraged," foreign investors will typically want to hold at least 51 percent ownership. The assumption is that with majority ownership comes control of the board. With control of the board comes control of the company. In China, however, there's an added wrinkle.

Instead of signatures, seals (commonly called "chops") bind contracts. Whoever's appointed representative director holds the company seal (as shown in Figure 2.4).

Figure 2.4 Example of company seal

Source: Courtesy of Dezan, Shira and Associates.

---

[31]J. Sheng and J. Zou. 2016. "China's Recent Restrictions on Outbound Investments by Chinese Companies," *Pillsbury.* www.pillsburylaw.com/en/news-and-insights/china-s-recent-restrictions-on-outbound-investments-by-chinese.html, (accessed September 27, 2018).

The representative director uses the company chop to approve all contracts and conduct all banking.

The budget request for a new packaging machine was approved. The foreign project manager was excited to get started on equipment purchases. After 2 months nothing had been bought.

Local buyers hadn't even received a single quote. It wasn't for lack of trying. They simply didn't know enough about packing equipment to find suppliers. The project manager spent the next 2 weeks writing a detailed Request for Quotation.

Within a month, three quotes arrived. A month after that, price negotiations were complete.

Not wanting to lose momentum, the project manager collected purchase order approval signatures himself.

A few weeks later, he contacted the machine builder to see how work was progressing. It wasn't. The vendor was waiting for the 20 percent prepayment specified in the PO. He reached out to his colleagues in Purchasing and Finance to find out what had happened.

"Why didn't anyone pay the vendor?"

"We never received an invoice."

"So it's their fault?"

"Actually, it's your fault. You only sent them a signed PO."

"What else do they need?"

"You needed to give the PO to Mr. Zhang's secretary before sending it to the vendor."

"What does Mr. Zhang's secretary have to do with POs?"

"Mr. Zhang is the company's representative director. His secretary is authorized by him to use the company seal on a PO of this amount. Without a company seal on the PO, the vendor couldn't do anything with it. So they never invoiced us."

With all legal authority resting with the representative director, operations need a system of checks and balances. One way to do this is for articles to specify that the representative director may serve as managing director (MD) but not also general manager (GM). In this way, if a change in leadership is needed, the board can appoint a new MD or instruct the MD to appoint a new GM.[32]

[When touring the warehouse facility, the representative director noticed a few changes.]

   "What's this?"

   "We started manufacturing parts."

   "I know we talked about making parts. I wasn't aware you were moving forward so quickly."

   "The increased revenue has really helped our bottom line."

   "That's true. But what about permits?"

   "We're in the process of filing for them."

   [A local lawyer later explained to the representative director that the business was still registered as a trading enterprise. It wasn't a manufacturer. Without the correct business license it wouldn't be possible to secure permits. He could be held liable for the illegal operation.]

When foreign investors have little to no experience in China, they'll more than likely hand GM responsibilities over to their Chinese partner. Over time it may become apparent that local management methods aren't meeting performance expectations. The local partner may blame problems on technology transferred. The foreign partner may counter that the problem isn't what's been transferred but how it's been managed. Conflicting expectations and management styles help explain why 50 percent of foreign-invested JVs in China fail.[33]

Given the poor odds of success, it's advisable to include a liquidation clause in JV articles. For example, if profits fall below an agreed amount for a specified period of time, the clause is invoked. The company board convenes for a vote. If the vote carries, liquidation steps spelled out in the

---

[32]Chinese companies are also required to have a board supervisor. The supervisor ensures the board is meeting and acting in accordance with articles.

[33]D. Harris. 2014. "How to Do a China Joint Venture. Take Your Sweet Time," *China Law Blog.* www.chinalawblog.com/2014/01/how-to-do-a-china-joint-venture-take-your-sweet-time.html, (accessed August 12, 2018).

articles are set in motion. Without such a clause "zombie firms" might be kept alive for years simply because no one can agree on how to kill them.

In light of these challenges, WOFEs are much more common in China than JVs. Across encouraged industries, they outnumber JVs nearly 10 to 1. WOFEs are classified by business type: Manufacturing WOFEs produce goods; consulting WOFEs perform services; and trading WOFEs operate wholesale or retail operations. In actuality, the lines of separation aren't always so clear. Some local authorities may consider labeling and packaging purchased parts to be manufacturing.[34]

When processing WOFE applications, it can be the case that local authorities have very specific development goals for areas under their supervision. Companies with questionable financing or those performing the "wrong" type of work may experience a number of bureaucratic hurdles.

Interestingly, the "right" place for almost 70 percent of foreign investment into China is through the former British colony of Hong Kong.[35] Terms of the territory's handover to Chinese authorities in 1997 involved "One Country Two Systems." In this arrangement, the Special Administrative Region is part of China but would retain its own currency and economic and legal systems through 2047. In 2020, mainland authorities imposed a new security law on the region. Interpretation and enforcement of this law fell to mainland personnel operating independently of local Hong Kong authorities. The Trump administration argued that such actions effectively ended "One Country, Two Systems." Under the Executive Order on Hong Kong Normalization and passage of the U.S. Hong Kong Autonomy Act in Congress:

- U.S. State Department no longer permits the sale of military equipment, high technology or dual use tech to Hong Kong.
- U.S. Commerce Department has suspended preferential treatment and export license exceptions for Hong Kong.

---

[34]Manufacturing WOFEs are permitted to buy and sell products made by their parent company.

[35]For a few hundred dollars, foreign investors can set up a Hong Kong company in a week. If that's too slow, online sellers can provide prenamed "shelf companies" for immediate use.

- U.S. Customs and Border Protection ruled that imports from Hong Kong must be labeled "Made in China," no longer "Made in Hong Kong."

Recent trade actions with the United States notwithstanding, Hong Kong's "Two systems" are still the case when looking at taxation. Mainland income tax on dividends paid to foreign investors can be as low as 0 or as high as 25 percent depending on amount invested, percentage foreign owned, and where dividends are sent.[33] When dividends are sent to the United States, the tax rate has been upward of 25 percent.[34] When dividends are sent to Hong Kong, if investors own more than 25 percent of mainland businesses, the tax rate has been as low as 10 percent. If Hong Kong investors own more than 25 percent of mainland businesses, the tax rate has been as low as 5 percent.

Besides taxes, there are additional challenges in moving profits out of China. As of 2019, FIEs can't pay any foreign dividends until all prior years' losses have been offset. In other words, if an operation accumulated $10 million in losses before turning a profit, profits would need to exceed $10 million before any foreign dividends could be paid.

Assuming FIEs meet profitability requirements, there may be additional issues when it comes to paying foreign dividends. Statutes no longer require minimum registered capital amounts by industry. But if actual investment falls below 50 percent of registered capital, as specified in articles, 10 percent of net profits must be paid into a reserve account before foreign dividends can be paid.

Given the cost and complexity of moving profits out of China, foreign investors might be tempted to lend rather than invest in operations. If loans originate from Hong Kong, there's no Hong Kong tax on the principal or interest paid because income was generated outside Hong Kong. Care, however, must be taken to ensure that the total amount of debt doesn't exceed total investment as specified in company articles. In lieu of a loan, investors might try to move money off the mainland by paying for foreign services. In this arrangement, the mainland operation pays 5 percent business tax on Hong Kong services provided. Once funds are in Hong Kong, the first $256,000 is taxed at 8.25 percent. Any additional income is taxed at 16.5 percent.[36]

When working with Hong Kong dollars, there's no limit on how much can be sent abroad. The same can't be said for transferring money off the mainland. The Chinese RMB isn't freely convertible. As of 2019, the State Administration of Foreign Exchange (SAFE) regulates how much a company can convert into foreign currency. It also regulates how much foreign currency a company can transfer out of China. Interestingly, as of 2020, China is piloting a digital RMB across four cities, with transactions exceeding $300 million. Goldman Sachs predicts that over the next 10 years digital RMB will account for 15 percent of total consumption payments.[37] China's attraction to central bank digital currency is twofold. On the one hand, a digital RMB would break the U.S. dollar monopoly on international transactions, but on the other hand, it "would give Beijing an unprecedented amount of information about how and where people are, and what they're spending their money on."[38] Whichever form of payment is being used in China, without a well-thought-out strategy for repatriating profits, managers can quickly find regulations ensure any money earned in China stays in China.

---

[36]P. Dwyer. 2018. "Hong Kong's New Two-tiered Profits Tax," *China Briefing*. www.china-briefing.com/news/hong-kongs-two-tiered-profits-tax/, (accessed September 20, 2019).

[37]N. DiCamillo. 2020. "China's Xi Asks G20 Countries to Be 'Open and Accommodating' to CBDCs," https://finance.yahoo.com/news/china-xi-asks-g20-countries-201613785.html, (accessed January 3, 2021).

[38]L. He. 2020. "China wants to weaponize its currency. A digital version could help," *CNN*.   https://www.cnn.com/2020/12/04/economy/china-digital-yuan-currency-intl-hnk/index.html, (accessed on February 22, 2021).

CHAPTER 3

Factory Construction

Local officials are responsible for processing business licenses, company articles of incorporation, and subsidies. This gives them tremendous influence over how foreign-invested enterprises (FIEs) are organized, what they make, how much they make, and even where they make it. For example, in February 2020, during the coronavirus outbreak, government officials nationalized an FIE producing surgical masks and put export restrictions in place.[1]

With regard to controlling where things are made, it's common for local officials to steer manufacturing operations into development zones. In 2011, there were 1,600 development zones in China.[2] By 2019 that number had climbed to 2,543. Today, China is home to more than half the world's development zones.[3]

With so many zones to choose from, which is best? It depends. There are 10 different types of economic development zones in China, the most popular of which are the following:

- special economic zones (SEZs)

---

[1]G. Chang. 2020. "Coronavirus Is Killing China's Factories (and Creating Economic Chaos)," *The National Interest.* https://nationalinterest.org/blog/buzz/coronavirus-killing-china%E2%80%99s-factories-and-creating-economic-chaos-126471, (accessed February 26, 2020).

[2]*China Briefing.* 2011. "Understanding Development Zones in China," www.china-briefing.com/news/2011/10/05/understanding-development-zones-in-china.html, (accessed September 19, 2018).

[3]D. Dodwell. 2019. "China is the World Leader in Special Economic Zones but the Results are Erratic at Best, With Many Being Underused or Failing to Benefit the Wider Economy," *South China Morning Post.* www.scmp.com/comment/opinion/article/3023067/china-world-leader-special-economic-zones-results-are-erratic-best, (accessed September 17, 2019).

- free trade zones (FTZs)
- economic and technological development zones (ETDZs)
- high-tech industrial development zones (HIDZs)

SEZs were the first. Four opened up along the southeastern coast in the early 1980s. Today, SEZs are located in 19 Chinese cities. As Figure 3.1 shows, all of these are located along the coast.

Figure 3.1 China's special economic zones

Source: Adapted by calling out SEZs on "Map of China en names.svg," by P. Potrowl, 2010, https://commons.wikimedia.org/wiki/File:Map_of_China_en_names.svg.

Besides benefiting from modern infrastructure and proximity to seaports, operations inside SEZs also enjoy lower income taxes. For example, as of 2019, Chinese companies pay upward of 13 percent business-to-business value-added tax (VAT) and 25 percent corporate income tax. Companies in SEZs might pay[4]:

---

[4]*China Unique.* 2019. "Special Economic Zones in China," http://chinaunique.com/business/sez.htm, (accessed March 23, 2019).

- 0 percent local tax
- 0 percent duty
- 0 percent income tax until profits are earned
- 0 percent income tax for the next 2 through 3 years
- Half the normal income tax for 2 additional years
- Standard rates thereafter

SEZs have proven so popular that they accounted for 22 percent of China's GDP, 45 percent of foreign direct investment, and 60 percent of exports in 2015.[5]

Building on this success, the state council introduced FTZs in 2013. Companies inside any one of China's 11 FTZs, as shown in Figure 3.2, enjoy bonded warehouses; 10 percent income tax; and relaxed rules on imports, exports, and foreign currency exchange.[6] The Shanghai Free Trade Zone has proven so popular that 3,633 enterprises registered within 3 months of its launch.[7]

With so many FTZs to choose from, which is best? It depends. With land and labor making up close to 70 percent of operating costs in China, FTZs in the western provinces of Chongqing, Shaanxi, and Sichuan are particularly well suited for large, vertically integrated operations.[8] On the other hand, labor-intensive operations with extensive, domestic, supply chains might prefer FTZs in the central provinces, where land and labor are cheaper than along the coast and logistics channels are more

---

[5]*China Development Bank*. 2015. "China's Special Economic Development Zones," www.worldbank.org/content/dam/Worldbank/Event/Africa/Investing%20in%20 Africa%20Forum/2015/investing-in-africa-forum-chinas-special-economic-zone. pdf, (accessed May 12, 2017).

[6]*HKTDC Research*. 2019. "China Pilot Free Trade Zones," http://china-trade-research. hktdc.com/business-news/article/Facts-and-Figures/China-Pilot-Free-Trade-Zones/ ff/en/1/1X000000/1X0A2V2D.htm, (accessed November 12, 2019).

[7]M. Zito. 2014. "Logistics, Warehousing and Transportation in China (Part 2)," *China Briefing*. www.china-briefing.com/news/logistics-warehousing-transportation- china-part-2/, (accessed November 17, 2018).

[8]S. Jones. 2011. "Operational Costs of Business in China's Inland Cities," *China Briefing*.   www.china-briefing.com/news/operational-costs-of-business-in-chinas- inland-cities/, (accessed November 12, 2018).

Figure 3.2 China's free trade zones

Source: Reprinted from "China Pilot Free Trade Zones," by HKTDC Research, 2019, http://china-trade-research.hktdc.com/business-news/article/Facts-and-Figures/China-Pilot-Free-Trade-Zones/ff/en/1/1X000000/1X0A2V2D.htm.

developed than in the west. Advanced manufacturing operations dependent on international supply chains tend to cluster along the coast, where the pool of high-skilled labor is larger, infrastructure is more up to date, and transportation costs are lower.

The cost of setting up operations in an SEZ may be out of reach for small manufacturers focused on light to medium industry. For these operations, the state council has established ETDZs. Unlike SEZs, which are based around large tier 1 cities, ETDZs are located in smaller tier 2 cities (and the suburbs of tier 1 cities). Although the infrastructure is less developed, costs are substantially lower. Table 3.1 lists China's 54 state-administrated ETDZs in 2016.[9]

---

[9]*China Internet Information Center.* 2016. "National Economic and Technical Development Zones," www.china.org.cn/english/features/etdz/75721.htm, (accessed November 19, 2018).

Table 3.1 State-administered ETDZs

Beijing	Guangzhou	Kunshan	Qingdao	Weihai	Yinchuan
Changchun	Guiyang	Lanzhou	Qinhuangdao	Wenzhou	Yingkou
Changsha	Hainan	Lhasa	Shanghai	Wuhan	Zhanjiang
Chengdu	Hangzhou	Lianyungang	Shenyang	Wuhu	Zhengzhou
Chongqing	Harbin	Nanchang	Shihezi	Xian	
Dalian	Hefei	Nanjing	Suzhou	Xiamen	
Dongshan	Hohhot	Nanning	Taiyuan	Xiaoshan	
Fuqing	Huizhou	Nantong	Tianjin	Xining	
Fuzhou	Kunming	Ningbo	Urumqi	Yantai	

By 2020, the number of ETDZs grew fourfold.[10] As the high rate of growth indicates, the majority of manufacturing in China is done by small- to medium-sized factories operating in local development zones.

What about operations involved in research and development (R&D)? Since 2012, China has been the worldwide leader in patents and trademarks.[11] As impressive as this sounds, it's important to remember that filing patents is one thing, but bringing them to market is something else. In 2016, an intellectual property management company examined 1,000 Chinese patents and found that less than 5 percent of them had any commercial potential. The same study found 50 percent of U.S. patents were commercially viable.[12]

---

[10]J. Percy. 2019. "Investing in China's Economic Development Zones," *China Briefing*. www.china-briefing.com/news/chinas-economic-development-zones-types-incentives/, (accessed January 19, 2019).

[11]*Hong Kong Means Business*. 2014. "China's Intellectual Property Development: New Dynamics and Opportunities'" http://hkmb.hktdc.com/en/1X09ZR7K/hktdc-research/China%E2%80%99s-Intellectual-Property-Development-New-Dynamics-and-Opportunities, (accessed September 19, 2018).

[12]S. Koch. 2016. "China's Dysfunctional Patent Flood," *Biocentury*. www.biocentury.com/bc-innovations/strategy/2016-11-21/how-poor-patents-hinder-tech-transfer-china, (accessed September 1, 2018).

To better commercialize R&D, the state council and the Ministry of Science and Technology have set up over 100 national-level HIDZs.[13] Companies inside HIDZs enjoy the following benefits: 15 percent corporate income tax, VAT exemption on R&D exports, VAT refund on R&D equipment purchases, and duty exemption on R&D imports. Companies will also receive discounts on overseas purchases if items are listed in the *Catalogue of Encouraged Imported Technology and Products*. In light of these perks, the number of companies setting up operations in HIDZs increased 60 percent every year from 1992 through 2005.[14] China now has its very own "Silicon Valley" in the city of Chengdu, where 83,000 companies recorded $20 billion in trade during 2017.[15]

For U.S.-based companies seeking to lower tax bills by setting up operations inside development zones, savings apply only if Chinese-generated income stays in China. Otherwise, U.S. corporate income tax is owed on repatriated profits. When the U.S. corporate income tax rate was cut from 35 percent to 20 percent in 2017, the Chinese Tax Bureau responded to the possible outflow of cash by exempting FIEs from withholdings tax if funds were reinvested in encouraged industries.

FIEs seeking tax exemptions and reduced income tax need to pay close attention to Chinese tax laws. Provisional income taxes must be filed monthly (or quarterly). Certified public accountants must sign off on accounts annually. Accounts can be particularly challenging for multinational companies (MNCs) involved in employing foreign support staff and/or subsidiaries. For example, foreigners working in China are required

---

[13]S. Liang. 2011."Physical Planning Strategies of National High Tech Industrial Development Zones in China," *University of Pennsylvania* 8th *Annual Urban Doctorate Symposium*. www.slideshare.net/PennUrbanResearch/physical-planning-strategies-of-national-hightechnology-industrial-development-zones-in-china, (accessed May 23, 2018).

[14]*China.org.cn*. 2006. "New and High Tech Development Zones," www.china.org.cn/english/features/Brief/192917.htm, (accessed February 21, 2017).

[15]Chengdu High Tech Development Zone. 2017. "Chengdu Hi-tech Industrial Development Zone (Chengdu Hi-tech Zone) Investing USD 730 Million to Attract Global Talent," *Cision PR Newswire*. www.prnewswire.com/news-releases/chengdu-hi-tech-industrial-development-zone-chengdu-hi-tech-zone--investing-usd-730-million-to-attract-global-talent-300405495.html, (accessed August 19, 2018).

to participate in social security plans. Plans jointly funded by employers and employees include pensions, medical insurance, and unemployment insurance. Plans funded solely by employers include workplace injury insurance and maternity insurance. Because plans are administrated at the provincial or municipal level, it can be the case that certain locations do not require foreigners to participate. Some countries (e.g., Germany, South Korea, Denmark, Canada, Finland, Switzerland, the Netherlands, Spain, Luxembourg, Japan, and Serbia) have signed social security agreements with China. Citizens of these countries working in China are eligible for social security exemptions. Regardless of country of origin, anyone working in China for more than 183 days in a year owes Chinese income tax. The tax bill is calculated on total global income (not just the amount paid while working in China). When it comes to transfer pricing between associated businesses, Chinese tax authorities require substantial amounts of documentation proving "arms' length" transfer pricing is being used. According to the *Enterprise Income Tax Law of 2008*, association is defined as companies sharing board members, 50 percent of debt, or 25 percent of ownership.[16]

Onerous tax regulations aren't the only reason operations keep their Chinese income inside China. Banking regulations also limit what they can do with their money. For example, in 2016, State Administration of Foreign Exchange (SAFE) cut the maximum amount that firms in China could send overseas from $50 million to $5 million.[17] Out-of-country payments were also limited to less than 30 percent of shareholders' equity.[18]

In light of low taxes, tight currency controls, and extensive banking regulations, operations managers can quickly find that the only real use

---

[16]*Deloitte*. 2009. "New Transfer Pricing Requirements in China," www2.deloitte.com/content/dam/Deloitte/cn/Documents/tax/deloitte-cn-tax-newtransferpricingrequirementsinchina-en-100609.pdf, (accessed February 20, 2020).

[17]J. Sheng and J. Zou. 2016. "China's Recent Restrictions on Outbound Investments by Chinese Companies," *Pillsbury*. www.pillsburylaw.com/en/news-and-insights/china-s-recent-restrictions-on-outbound-investments-by-chinese.html, (accessed September 27, 2018).

[18]G. Wildau, et al. 2016. "China limits gold imports and renminbi outflows," *Financial Times*. www.ft.com/content/cc6b5622-b79b-11e6-ba85-95d1533d9a62, (accessed August 2, 2018).

for local profits is reinvesting them in local operations. Incentivizing rein-vestment is key to China's development, particularly in the construction sector.

> *"Two of our suppliers recently opened up new factories nearby?"*
> *"It doesn't surprise me. Most of our suppliers have local facilities."*
> *"Do you think they move here to meet our short lead time requirements?"*
> *"Maybe. But it probably has more to do with government subsidies."*
> *"What do you mean?"*
> *"We make electric cars. The local government only offers tax breaks to our suppliers if they are local. So our big suppliers set up small, local workshops."*
> *"Is that efficient?"*
> *"I'm sure it's not. But margins in this industry are tight. Suppliers need the subsidies to survive."*
> *"What happens when subsidies are cut?"*
> *"They pick up their machines and move somewhere else."*
> *"Where?"*
> *"Wherever local governments give them enough subsidies."*

The top 60 Chinese builders control approximately 30 percent of the construction market. This gives builders a big advantage when negotiating construction terms. Another source of advantage is who they are. Of the top 10 contractors, seven are state-owned enterprises (SOEs). A high degree of state control also describes how factories are designed. Of the top 60 design firms, 50 are SOEs.

Given the state's dominant role in factory construction and design, it's little wonder that both sectors are heavily regulated. An argument could be made that regulations are needed to ensure factories are built according to safety standards, quality is maintained, and the environment is protected. The counterargument is that excessive regulation drives up construction costs, increases delays, reduces quality, and promotes corruption. In 2015, U.S.–China Business Council outlined the long and complex system of approvals and permits needed to initiate a wholly owned foreign enterprise (WOFE) construction project (Figure 3.3).[19]

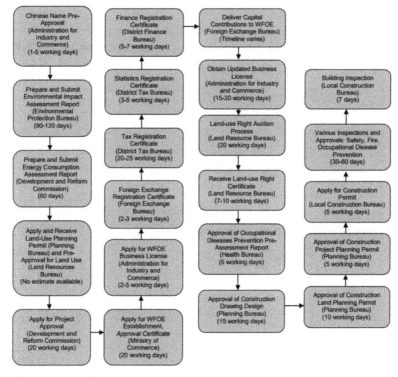

Source: Sidley Austin; Timelines are estimates

Figure 3.3 Timeline for a WOFE construction project

Source: Reprinted from "Licensing Challenges and Best Practices in China," by The US–China Business Council, 2014, www.uschina.org/sites/default/files/Licensing%20Challenges%20 and%20Best%20Practices%20in%20China-Jan%202014.pdf.

The construction approvals process typically starts with the management committee responsible for the development zone where construction will occur. If the business prospectus and scope of work are consistent

---

[19] *US China Business Council*. 2014. "Licensing Challenges and Best Practices in China," www.uschina.org/sites/default/files/Licensing-Jan2014.pdf, (accessed August 19, 2018).

with the committee's goals for the location, the application will likely be approved and make its way to the local economic development bureau (EDB).

EDB review starts with a feasibility report. This is a technical analysis of construction scope. Applicants can't write reports themselves. They need to hire locally licensed writers. Given the level of detail required, factory designers must be hired before feasibility reports can be written.

Like report writers, factory designers must also be licensed. Licenses are issued either at the municipal or at the provincial level, depending on what's being designed and where construction will occur. For example, piping layouts typically require municipal licenses. Licenses vary depending on what's being piped (clean water, waste water, compressed air, volatile gases, steam, etc.).

It's highly unlikely that one design firm will have all the necessary licenses to design everything in construction scope. As a result, designers subcontract tasks to other designers. With so many parties involved, delays, mistakes, and confusion are commonplace.

"These drawings are wrong. I asked for the ground and neutral wires to be separated."

"In China we typically combined them. It's cheaper."

"I know. But it can cause hysteresis in the power lines, which can damage my equipment. Please change."

[2 weeks pass]

"When can I see the new wiring drawings?"

"They'll be done next week."

[A week passes]

"Where are the new drawings?"

"They'll arrive tomorrow."

[Tomorrow comes and goes and still no drawings.]

"Where are the drawings you promised?"

"Something came up. You should have them in 2 weeks."

"That's unacceptable! Yesterday, you said the drawings would be here today. Now you say 'wait another 2 weeks.' What's going on?"

"We aren't actually creating your wiring drawings. Our partner's doing the work. They're very busy. Anyway, they recommend keeping the ground and neutral wires combined. Everybody does it. It's cheaper."

Further complicating factory design is determining the level of detail needed for feasibility reports. Drawings need to be specific enough to meet EDB requirements but not too detailed; otherwise, time and money are wasted if reports are rejected. To ensure feasibility reports have the right amount of detail, the local EDB might recommend writers and designers. Unfortunately, these firms are typically the most expensive.

If factory designs call out additional transformer capacity is needed, the approvals process becomes more complex. The local power bureau will need to determine whether the power request meets National Development and Reform Commission (NDRC) guidelines for energy efficiency. If approved, the factory will pay per kilowatt hour of electricity consumed plus a fixed, monthly amount per kilowatt of transformer capacity installed. Even when factories are operating within their approved power levels, they could experience power cuts. The issue is supply and demand.

Nearly 70 percent of China's energy is consumed by six sectors:

1. Electricity generation
2. Steel manufacturing
3. Nonferrous metal processing
4. Construction materials
5. Oil processing
6. Chemicals

When their demand for power peaks, operations in other sectors may experience power rationing or cuts. The issue is coal. Over 70 percent of China's electricity is generated by burning coal. Coal prices change with the market, whereas electricity prices don't. They're set by the NDRC. For example, in 2011, when coal prices rose 80 percent, the NDRC increased electricity prices only 15 percent, the intention being to control inflation. Unfortunately, low electricity prices and high coal costs meant that the more power generated, the more money power stations lost. In 2018, 40 percent of China's coal-fired power stations lost money.[20]

---

[20]S. Ambrogi. 2018. "40% of China's Coal Power Stations Are Losing Money," *Carbon Tracker*. www.carbontracker.org/40-of-chinas-coal-power-stations-are-losing-money/, (accessed August 20, 2019).

[The local power bureau notified the factory manager that electricity to his plant would be cut sometime in the next 3 hours. He couldn't accept this. He went to the power station to see what could be done.]

"Due to the recent heat wave we can't produce enough power. We have to cut your electricity."

"If demand's so high why is one of your generators offline?"

"We're doing maintenance."

"Who schedules maintenance during a heat wave?"

"Someone who can't afford to generate any more power."

When power cuts happen, factory managers can find their operations are affected for hours, days, or even weeks. To add to their frustration, a fixed portion of electric bills remains unchanged during cuts.

If factory management can't tolerate power disruptions, installing backup, diesel generators is an option. However, this isn't a quick or easy fix. Time from plan submission to final approval can take anywhere from 4 to 6 months. After factoring in maintenance, operating, and diesel costs, factory generated power can be anywhere from three to four times more expensive than city power.

When discussing power issues with local officials, it's important to remember that many decisions are outside their control. For example, the National Energy Commission (NEC) writes national energy policy. A national policy of particular importance to local power bureaus is lowering energy consumption per unit of production.[21]

Once a week, the company trucked in liquid nitrogen from a distributor 200 miles away. To cut costs and the facility's carbon footprint, management wanted to generate nitrogen gas on site.

The local power bureau agreed generating gas would benefit the company and the environment. But it would also require additional power to run the generator. The added power wouldn't translate into increased production. Since the NEC measures energy efficiency as power consumed per unit produced, the plan was deemed inefficient and rejected.

---

[21]The goal is 16 percent reduction in power per unit of GDP using 2012 as a baseline.

Assuming the local EBD and power bureau approve a feasibility report, the next step is submitting a job safety assessment report to the workers safety bureau (WSB). The report details what, if any, dangerous activities will be performed during factory construction and how these risks will be managed. As with feasibility reports, applicants can't write their own safety assessment reports. They must be prepared by locally licensed writers.

In addition to a job safety assessment report, applicants will also need to file an environmental impact assessment (EIA) report with the local EPB. Although EIA report content isn't standardized, China's Environmental Protection (EP) Law recommends that reports answer the following questions:

- What are environmental conditions at the site prior to the start of construction?
- What type of business will be done once construction is complete?
- How many people will be employed?
- What will be made?
- How much will be made?
- What equipment, materials, and processes will be used?
- How much waste will be generated?
- How will waste be treated?
- Can treatment methods meet environmental standards?

Similarly to the case with all other construction reports, applicants can't write their own EIAs. They must be prepared by writers licensed by the local EPB, which decides on EIA scope and approves reports. For example, if construction involves expanding a factory, the local EPB determines whether an addendum to an existing EIA will suffice or a new EIA is needed. An addendum is generally preferred because it restricts EIA evaluation to the area of new construction. If a new EIA is needed, the entire facility must be reevaluated. Because China's environmental laws (and local EPB interpretations of these laws) frequently change, reevaluations typically require substantial facility updates.

Once the feasibility report, EIA report, energy use report, and workers safety reports are all filed and approved, applications can proceed to land bureau registration.

The local land bureau will need to issue a land use right certificate. This certificate gives users the right to perform specific tasks on the land for a defined period. Factory land use rights are typically for 30 years. During this time factory owners can sell rights, but land use as described in certificates can be changed only at the ministerial level.

In addition to securing land use rights, applicants will also need a geological report. This report provides details about the water table, ecology, soil weight-bearing capacity, and possible pollutants at the construction site. As with all the other reports, only locally licensed writers can prepare geological reports.

With an approved geological report in hand, construction plans can be filed with the local tax, finance, and statistics bureaus, which ensure taxes are being paid, land use is accounted for, and total investment is recorded. Business registration bureau approval may also be needed if, as a result of construction business, activities change. If new business activities involve foreign trade, the import and export bureau must approve the request.

Once all government reports and bureau notifications are filed, registered, and approved, detailed design work on the factory can finally begin. Design work is relatively simple if the factory, as shown in Figure 3.4, resembles what's typically built in the area.

Figure 3.4 Typical Chinese factory

Source: Courtesy of Peng Zhiqiang.

Officials from at least a dozen government bureaus will need to review factory designs. These bureaus include the following:

1. Fire bureau
2. Health bureau
3. Labor bureau
4. Planning bureau
5. Construction bureau
6. Construction quality inspection bureau
7. Construction safety bureau
8. Power bureau
9. Water bureau
10. gas bureau
11. telephone bureau
12. traffic bureau

Local officials are able to quickly approve only factory designs that they're accustomed to seeing. Anything unique or incorporating imported equipment will typically take much longer to approve. Depending on how many drawing revisions are required, approvals can take anywhere from 2 to 6 months. Only after approvals are given is it possible to bid contractors.[22]

It's common practice to use locally licensed auditors when selecting contractors. Auditors know local construction costs. This allows them to weed out contractors who are over- or underbidding. Auditors aren't finished once contractors are selected. During the build, they check whether brands and quantities used match designs. They also send building material samples out for quality testing.

In addition to hiring auditors, companies might hire a supervision firm. Supervisors oversee contractors to ensure that the following conditions are met:

- The right people are in the right places doing the right jobs at the right times.

---

[22]Contractors can build using only drawings that carry seals from licensed designers and government approvers.

- Milestone completion dates specified in the purchase agreement are met.
- National, provincial, and local safety standards are followed.

Auditors and supervisors are typically paid a flat fee for their work. Bonuses might be paid for uncovering quality issues or meeting build schedules. Auditors are also paid to produce an audit book. The supervision company presents this book to government officials as evidence that construction quantities, materials, and methods matched what was approved.

The supervision company will also follow up with the provincial survey commission. The commission is responsible for performing a survey of the build site for the land bureau. The land bureau is ultimately responsible for approving factory occupancy.[23]

Clearly, construction in China has many issues. For starters, the same agencies that license report writers, designers, auditors, and supervisors also approve their work. It is therefore possible that the case approvals are based more on connections than on the quality of work done.

Another issue is bureaucracy. In 2018, the General Office of the State Council issued a pilot reform of engineering construction projects approval. The goal was to simplify the approvals process by combining multiple governmental approvals into a more unified system.[24] As of 2020, reforms haven't been rolled out.

To add to the complexity of construction, owners don't actually own the land on which their factories sit. Land in China hasn't been privately owned since the Party came to power in 1949. Rural land is owned by village collectives.[25] Urban land is owned by the state. Factories can be built only on urban land leased from local governments.

---

[23]While awaiting land bureau approval, factories can be used for a 6-month probationary period.

[24]E. Yan and B. Lui. 2019. "Construction and Projects in China: An Overview," *Thomson Reuters: Practical Law.* https://content.next.westlaw.com/2-521-5363?transitionType=Default&contextData=(sc.Default)&__lrTS=20191129202942907, (accessed February 10, 2020).

[25]While collectives own land, they can't sell it. Nor can they use it for purposes other than farming.

Local governments need factory investment because their budgets are highly dependent on land lease revenues. For example, unlike VAT, in which 75 percent of receipts are sent back to the central government, local governments keep 100 percent of land lease payments. Leasing land generates a substantial amount of money considering real estate and construction make up roughly 30 percent of China's economic output. However, lease payments aren't the only revenue stream from land development. Local governments can also earn a lot of money from investing in development projects.

Prior to 2014, it was illegal for local governments to borrow money. Part of the reason was to prevent officials from speculating on land development. Local governments could, however, form urban development and construction companies. These SOEs have borrowed heavily to invest in construction projects. In 2010, China's National Audit Office estimated local governments had accumulated close to $2 trillion in debt. Nearly 80 percent of this debt was in land development projects.[26] Local governments are using land lease payments to service almost 40 percent of their debt. Debt is structured such that in 2020 Chinese developers had close to $65 billion in aggregate bond payments due[27]. The problem with such a high dependence on land leases is availability of land to lease.

China has over 1.3 billion people to feed in a country where only 15 percent of the land is suitable for agriculture. Unfortunately, most of the fertile land is along the coast, where thousands of economic development zones are located. To protect the food supply, provincial and ministerial land bureaus set strict quotas for local governments specifying the following:

- Maximum amounts of rural land that can be converted into urban land

---

[26]D. Davis and D. McMahon. 2013. "Xi faces Test over China's Local Debt," *The Wall Street Journal.* www.wsj.com/articles/china-local-government-debt-surges-to-3-trillion-1388395467, (accessed July 16, 2018).

[27]P. Liu. 2020. "Evergrande Slashes Property Prices by 30 per cent across China for One Month, Sounding Clarion Call on Discount War," *The South China Morning Post.* https://www.scmp.com/business/china-business/article/3100510/evergrande-sounds-clarion-property-price-war-chinas-biggest, (accessed Sept. 9, 2020).

- Minimum amounts of rural land that must be maintained
- Maximum amounts of urban land that can be under development

Company executives hoping to build factories need to be very wary of local officials promising to do so on rural land. Land reclassification can happen only at the ministerial level.

A foreign investor wanted to acquire a Chinese factory. On paper everything looked great. The price was reasonable; financials were strong; growth prospects were good; and the owner wanted to sell.

As part of due diligence, a local civil engineering firm performed a site review. There were a number of glaring building code violations. Permit searches at the local land, construction, and planning bureaus showed the factory had never been cited for violations because it didn't officially exist. The facility was illegally built on rural land. Acquisition was impossible.

As available lots become scarcer, owners of existing residences or factories can find themselves being relocated to make room for new development.

Over the years, the city grew. Factories that were once outside of town were now surrounded by it. Residents routinely complained to local officials about factory noise, traffic, and pollution. Eventually, an ordinance was passed making it illegal for large trucks to enter or leave the city between the hours of 6 am and 10 pm.

Most businesses took the hint and relocated. A few held out, trying to negotiate better lease buyout terms with the city. As the inventory of unsold apartments grew, local officials couldn't find developers willing to pay enough to cover the cost of relocating the remaining factories.

These companies were stuck. On the one hand, the government couldn't afford to move them. On the other hand, it didn't make sense for them to maintain facilities that would be torn down as soon as the city found a developer.

What options do owners have once officials have earmarked their properties like the one shown in Figure 3.5 for demolition? Not many once the symbol to tear down (as shown in Figure 3.6) is painted on the building.

Figure 3.5 Factory to be torn down

Source: Courtesy of Xubiao Wu.

Figure 3.6 Chinese character designating a building for demolition

Source: Courtesy of Xubiao Wu.

Local officials might offer factory owners cash to leave. The amount, however, may not be enough to move equipment and build a new factory. In lieu of cash, officials might offer to build a new factory. Unfortunately, government-built factories are generally made to a lower quality standard in areas unable to attract investment.

Whenever and wherever factories are built, delays are common. A big part of the problem is the approximately 12 government agencies and five government reports required. The wheels of bureaucracy turn very slowly. In the past, to make up for lost time, environment protections all too often fell by the wayside.

By 2002 China was home to six of the world's 10 most polluted cities. That same year, 75 percent of the water in rivers flowing through Chinese cities was unsuitable for drinking or fishing.[28] How was pollution on such a level possible? After all, municipal planning departments can't approve construction drawings for bidding until local EPB officials have signed off on EIA reports.

Management wanted to install three new production lines in the factory. Because of this investment, capacity would exceed what was listed in the EIA report. The local EPB required a new EIA for the facility.

The EIA writer discovered many areas of noncompliance. Exhaust pipes didn't extend high enough above the roof line, ventilation fans didn't have carbon filters, and storage racks weren't to code.

Management disagreed with report findings. None of the issues had anything to do with the new production lines.

The EIA writer explained laws had changed since the plant was built 6 years ago. The entire facility needed to be in compliance with the latest regulations.

---

[28]M. Krzysztof and E. Mazur. 2006. "Environmental Compliance and Enforcement in China: An Assessment of Current Practices and Ways Forward," *Organization for Economic Co-Operation and Development.* www.oecd.org/environment/outreach/37867511.pdf, (accessed May 12, 2017).

In reality, the local EPB is funded by the local EDB. Construction projects favored by the EDB might receive preferential treatment by the EPB. By the same token, if EDB officials don't want particular investments to happen, EIAs might never be approved regardless of environmental impact. It could be argued that prior to 2015 the EPB was free to protect the environment so long as its efforts didn't get in the way of development. Fines were capped, and EPB officials didn't have the right to seize polluting assets. For example, it might cost 500,000 RMB per year to operate in compliance with environmental standards. But the fee for ignoring regulations might be only 10,000 RMB.

Clearly, the policy of prioritizing development over the environment wasn't sustainable. The National People's Congress approved revisions to China's EP Law in 2015. Polluting factories for the first time face:

- Cumulative fines with no limits
- Permanent closure or temporary suspension of operations
- Criminal charges that can result in detention of managers

[The plant general manager and EHS manager were having a disagreement about waste water treatment.]

"We need to start treating our own waste water."

"Why? We're having it treated by a 3rd party?"

"I know. But we need to treat it ourselves."

"Our discharge volume is small. It doesn't makes sense to invest in a treatment system."

"It may not make economic sense, but it's needed for compliance."

"Why? As long as our waste water's being treated, who cares who treats it?"

"Our EIA says we treat our waste water."

"We wrote that back when we thought plant output would be higher. Until production picks up, it makes more sense to outsource treatment."

"If our EIA report had said our waste water would be treated, outsourcing would be fine. But our EIA says we treat our own waste water. So we have to treat it."

"What if we don't?"

"The local EPB can shut us down."

New factory construction is increasingly judged against national "green" deliverables. In the 11th Five Year Plan (2006 through 2010), the NDRC called for reducing water consumption per unit of industrial value add by 30 percent, reducing energy intensity by 20 percent, and increasing recycling on industrial solid waste by 60 percent.[29] At the same time, China's Ministry of Construction launched a green building evaluation standard. The standard rates new construction across six categories:

1. land savings and outdoor environment
2. energy savings
3. water savings
4. materials savings
5. indoor environmental quality
6. operations and management

As a result of these efforts as well as (1) forbidding the burning of coal inside city limits, (2) closing thousands of polluting factories, and (3) restricting heavy truck traffic in urban areas, China's average annual concentration of airborne pollutants (termed PM2.5) decreased almost 60 percent from the level in 2010.[30] By 2018 none of the world's 10 most polluted cities were in China.[31] The goal, by 2030, is to reduce Chinese carbon dioxide emissions by at least 65 percent compared with

[29]M. Krzysztof and E. Mazur. 2006. "Environmental Compliance and Enforcement in China: An Assessment of Current Practices and Ways Forward," *Organization for Economic Co-Operation and Development*. www.oecd.org/environment/outreach/37867511.pdf, (accessed May 12, 2017).

[30]G. Shih. 2019. "Beijing Air Improves Significantly in Past Five Years, Study Finds," *The Washington Post*. www.washingtonpost.com/world/asia_pacific/beijing-air-improves-dramatically-in-last-five-years-study-finds/2019/09/12/1b64028e-d54d-11e9-ab26-e6dbebac45d3_story.html, (accessed February 10, 2020).

[31]J. Griffiths. 2019. "22 of the Top 30 Most Polluted Cities in the World are in India," *CNN*. www.cnn.com/2019/03/04/health/most-polluted-cities-india-china-intl/index.html, (accessed February 1, 2020).

2005 levels. By 2060, the Party aims to install sufficient green power generation to be carbon neutral.[32]

It could be said that through new laws and regulations, China will be able to significantly reduce the environmental impact of development. The counterargument is that when faced with new laws, companies will simply be less open about disclosing environmental impact. For example, a recent report indicated that 98 percent of the 142 Chinese companies analyzed failed to meet even half of the minimum climate risk disclosure standards.[33] Another way to hide impact is to make improvements in one location at the expense of others. As of 2018, six of the 10 most polluted cities in China are in Hebei province. Hebei is the country's largest steel producing region.[34] Pollution control measures have failed to address how steel is made. The same approach could be said to describe how buildings are made.

About 2 billion square meters of new buildings were under construction in China during 2012. Yet only 10 buildings applied for recognition under China's national three-star green building rating system.[35] By 2020, China's national climate commitment was calling for 50 percent of all new buildings constructed to be certified green.[36] The problem with implementing such sweeping reforms is that so many Chinese structures, such as the one shown in Figure 3.7, aren't built so much as poured.

---

[32]S. Tan. 2021. "China's Carbon Neutral 'Transformation' Could Cost US$6.4 Trillion, But Plan Has 'Achilles' Heel'," *South China Morning Post.* https://www.scmp.com/economy/china-economy/article/3125904/chinas-carbon-neutral-transformation-could-cost-us64-trillion, (accessed March 21, 2021).

[33]E. Ng. 2020. "Chinese Companies Must Step Up with Climate Disclosures as They Fail to Meet Even Half the Minimum Standards, LGIM Says," *South China Morning Post.* https://www.scmp.com/business/companies/article/3113818/chinese-companies-must-step-climate-disclosures-they-fail-meet, (accessed January 23, 2021).

[34]*Reuters.* 2018. "Air Quality Worsening in China's Yangtze River Delta in 2018, Figures Show," www.scmp.com/news/china/policies-politics/article/2147410/air-quality-worsening-chinas-yangtze-river-delta-2018, (accessed January 30, 2020).

[35]C. Larson. 2012. "The Cracks in China's Shiny Buildings," *Bloomberg.* www.bloomberg.com/news/articles/2012-09-27/the-cracks-in-chinas-shiny-buildings, (accessed July 7, 2018).

[36]D. Weyl and M. Hong. 2017. "Lessons from China's Ambitious Green Building Movement," *GreenBiz.* https://www.greenbiz.com/article/lessons-chinas-ambitious-green-building-movement#:~:text=China%20has%20grand%20plans%20to,Year%20Plan%20prioritizes%20building%20efficiency, (accessed Sept 9, 2020).

Figure 3.7 Typical all-cement building construction

Source: Courtesy of Xubiao Wu.

Every three and a half years China pours more cement than the United States did during the entire twentieth century. To make all this cement, close to two billion tons of limestone is crushed, milled, and ground annually, putting a tremendous amount of dust and carbon dioxide into the air. In 2018, China's building sector accounted for approximately 20 percent of the country's total energy consumption and 25 percent of greenhouse gas emissions.[37] Sustainability requires that

---

[37]W. Feng, et al. 2018. "Constructing a New Low-Carbon Future: How Chinese Cities Are Scaling Ambitious Building Energy Efficient Solutions," *C40 China Buildings Programme: Launch Report*. www.c40.org/researches/constructing-a-new-low-carbon-future-china, (accessed February 11, 2020).

building regulators, designers, report writers, contractors, auditors, supervisors, and operations managers rethink factory construction in China. One way local governments are promoting new construction methods is through financial incentives. For example, in Wuxi, buildings that achieve a three-star green building rating are eligible for a $75,000 stipend from the district government.

CHAPTER 4

Labor

Once a factory is built, the next key challenge is making sure it's adequately staffed. Chinese operations typically employ a large number of people, as Figure 4.1 shows.

Figure 4.1 Labor-intensive manufacturing

Source: Courtesy of Peng Zhiqiang.

In 2009 roughly 112 million people worked in Chinese factories.[1] That means roughly one out of every four members of China's workforce (excluding agriculture) is employed in manufacturing. Chinese factories account for half of all people working in manufacturing globally.[2]

The project manager accepted a 3-year assignment in China. With local government health check complete, work and residence permits in place, driver hired, accommodations arranged, bank account opened, police registration submitted, and translator on board, he was finally ready to start working.

A number of areas in the factory were in need of attention. A worker attempting to clean an overhead light without proper safety equipment seemed like a good place to start.

"Mr. Zhang, your maintenance worker needs to be wearing a safety harness."

"No problem. He's done this before."

"That's not the point. Company rules require him to wear a harness when working at such a height."

"Ok. I'll tell him to get one." [An hour later the worker returns without a harness]

"He couldn't find one. It probably broke and no one replaced it."

"Please ask Mr. Liu in the purchasing dept. to buy one." [Another day passes]

"Mr. Zhang, do you have the new harness?"

"Mr. Liu's still getting quotes."

[Two more days pass]

"Do you have the harness now?"

"Mr. Liu's negotiating price."

---

[1]C. Mike. 2020. "Chinese Manufacturing: Fascinating Facts and Figures," *China Mike.* www.china-mike.com/facts-about-china/manufacturing-chinese-workforce/, (accessed February 11, 2020).

[2]J. Banister. 2005. "Manufacturing Employment and Compensation in China," *Beijing Javelin Investment Consulting Group.* www.bls.gov/fls/chinareport.pdf, (accessed March 16, 2018).

[A few days later the harness arrives]

"Mr. Zhang, when will your worker use the new harness to clean the light?"

"The harness wasn't GB certified.[1] Mr. Yang in the health and safety dept. said we couldn't use it. Purchasing will arrange a different one."

[Two days pass]

"Mr. Zhang, has the certified harness arrived yet?"

"We have another problem. Since the harness will be used to clean a light in workshop #1, that department's manager needs to sign off on the purchase request. He said the GB-certified harness is too expensive."

[After 2 hours of explaining the need for a certified harness, the department manager relents and signs the requisition order. Mr. Zhang promises that the new harness will be used to clean the light. The next day the light is clean.]

"I'm so happy to see that you used the new harness to clean the light?"

"Actually, the light broke on 2nd shift, so we took it down and put up a new bulb."

"Well, at least you used the harness."

"Mr. Liu bought the harness like you asked. Since you were so upset when the last harness was returned, he put the new harnesses on your desk so you could see it when you arrived at work. Unfortunately, your office was locked last night when the light broke."

"What happened?"

"We wanted to wait, but the supervisor complained that the shop was too dark. So the repairman changed the light without using the harness."

[Dejected, the project manager walked back to his office thinking, "How am I going to work in China when I can't even manage something as simple as changing a light bulb?" Just then he noticed a worker standing in his office. The worker was wearing the harness cleaning the broken light. True to his word, Mr. Zhang made sure the harness was used to clean the bulb.]

---

[1]GB (Guo Biao) is the Chinese national quality standard.

When visiting at a typical Chinese factory, it can seem as if people are everywhere. Most of them will be involved in production or finished product inspection. Many will be engineers. In 2005 a Duke University study estimated that Chinese universities graduate some 350,000 engineers per year. That's three times the number of U.S. engineering graduates.[3]

> *The foreign engineer was accustomed to working in factories with a lot of machines and few people. Here, the opposite was true. Chinese workers easily outnumbered equipment.*
>
> *He noticed most workers spent their days loading and unloading machines. A few, higher skilled workers handled machine setups and adjustments.*
>
> *Just when he thought he'd seen everyone, he was escorted to another room. Here he observed what could only be described as a sea of people. Row after row of inspectors sat at desks checking every part made in the factory.*
>
> *Noticing his shock, the shift supervisor laughed. "In China, we have many people. Your job is figuring out how we use them to make good parts."*
>
> *"That sounds difficult."*
>
> *"Don't worry. If something goes wrong, the inspectors will probably find it."*
>
> *Obviously, nothing in his training or experience had prepared him for this.*

When staffing factories, a key consideration is whether or not candidates are legally able to work. In 2011 there were approximately 250 million migrant workers in China.[4] In other words, one out of every two nonfarm workers in China are migrants. Who are these migrants? For thousands of years, local Chinese authorities have managed the movement of citizens through a system of household registrations (called *hukou*). Figure 4.2 is an example of a *hukou*.

---

[3]G. Bracey. 2006. "Heard the One about 600,000 Chinese Engineers?" *Washington Post.com.* www.washingtonpost.com/wp-dyn/content/article/2006/05/19/AR2006051901760.html, (accessed May 18, 2018).

[4]L. Hinnant and B. Janssen. November, 2018. "A Growing Toll: 56,800 Migrants Dead and Missing in 4 Years," *AP News.*

Figure 4.2 Chinese hukou

Source: Courtesy of Xubiao Wu.

Citizens have access to housing, work, health care, pensions, public education, and marriage licenses only in their *hukou* area. Migrants live or work outside their *hukou* area. A typical reason is to escape poverty in the countryside. So many people have left the countryside that China's urban workforce grew by 6 percent from 2000 through 2012.[5] For the first time in history, more Chinese people are living in cities than in the countryside.

The foreign parent company had been operating a wholly owned subsidiary in China for the past 10 years. Recently, a second factory was opened in another province. The new factory was having many start-up problems.

Headquarters offered some experienced staff in its original factory promotions to work in the new factory. Very few people took the offer. When asked why, typical responses were as follows:

"My child is in a good high school. With the national college entrance exam only a few years away, changing schools isn't possible."

"My parents are retired. They live with my family. I don't make enough money to move everyone."

---

[5]J. Xue and W. Gao. 2012. "How Large Is the Urban-Rural Income Gap in China?" *China Economic Policy Review.* http://faculty.washington.edu/karyiu/confer/sea12/papers/SC12-110%20Xue_Guo.pdf, (accessed July 12, 2018).

In recent years, calls to end the *hukou* system have been mounting. A commonly cited reason is that an urban-based society shouldn't need to tie people to the land of their birthplace. Others, however, support the *hukou* system. They argue that providing benefits to China's 250 million or so migrants throughout their working lives could cost upward of $3.7 trillion.[6] With almost 70 percent of Chinese factories located in small towns and villages, this cost would fall primarily on small manufacturers.

The owner of a family-owned company on the outskirts of town built a dormitory adjacent to his factory. When asked why, he explained, "My factory makes very simple products. To keep prices low, I hire migrants and pay them very little. I have to house them because they can't afford apartments in town. If they don't like the work, wages or living conditions, they can quit. There's always someone else willing to take their place."

Even though Chinese wages are among the world's lowest, labor is still a primary cost when manufacturing in China. The reasons are that Chinese factories tend to employ a large number of people and employers are responsible for contributing to a host of social security funds (e.g., pensions, medical, unemployment, work-related injury, and maternity). In terms of the number of people employed, most of those in the industrial sector work in privately owned companies. This is a relatively recent development. For example, from 2005 through 2015 state-owned enterprise (SOE) employment decreased from 27 percent of the workforce to 18 percent.[7] By 2017 the private sector accounted for roughly 90 percent of new jobs.[8] A lot of these private sector, industrial jobs are low

---

[6]K. Chan. 2013. "A Road Map for Reforming China's Hukou System," *China Dialogue*. www.chinadialogue.net/article/show/single/en/6432-A-road-map-for-reforming-China-s-hukou-system, (accessed July 15, 2018).

[7]C. Zhang. 2019. "How Much Do State-Owned Enterprises Contribute to China's GDP and Employment?" *The World Bank*. http://documents.worldbank.org/curated/en/449701565248091726/pdf/How-Much-Do-State-Owned-Enterprises-Contribute-to-China-s-GDP-and-Employment.pdf, (accessed January 5, 2020).

[8]A. Guluzade. 2019. "Explained, the Role of China's State-Owned Companies," *World Economic Forum*. www.weforum.org/agenda/2019/05/why-chinas-state-owned-companies-still-have-a-key-role-to-play/, (accessed February 11, 2020).

paying ($1.75 per hour). They also tend to involve producing high volumes of low-priced commodities for export.[9] A problem with this approach is labor inefficiency. In the United States approximately 12 million workers produce 19 percent of the world's output. For only 6 percent more output, manufacturers in China employ over ten times more people. Inefficiency isn't the result of effort. Under a "996" work culture Chinese tech workers are known for working from 9 a.m. to 9 p.m. 6 days a week. Ironically, the productivity problem is that employees are seldom in their jobs long enough to become very good at them. It isn't unusual for operations managers in China to find that 5 to 10 percent of their workforce quits every year. In 2019 the Labor Department in Dongguan, Guangdong province, reported that some 800 factories expect to be short by 100,000 staff.[10] With official unemployment at 5 percent in 2018, as jobs go unfilled recruitment becomes less about finding the right people than about finding any people.[11]

The factory employed 500 people. Each month 10 to 20 workers left. So many people were quitting that management had no idea from week to week if there would be enough workers to fill production orders. During a particularly bad week, the plant manager asked, "In a country with over a billion people, why can't we find workers?"

The Human Resources (HR) manager explained, "For each open position, we send job descriptions to two or three local employment agencies. Within a week they'll give us eight resumes.

[9]C. Mike. 2020. "Chinese Manufacturing: Fascinating Facts and Figures," *China Mike.* www.china-mike.com/facts-about-china/manufacturing-chinese-workforce/, (accessed February 11, 2020).

[10]H. Huifeng. 2019. "China's Factories Struggling to Find Young Staff as Young Migrant Workers Seek 'Freedom' in the Service Sector," *South China Morning Post.* www.scmp.com/news/china/society/article/2187501/chinese-factories-struggle-find-staff-migrant-workers-look, (accessed February 10, 2020).

[11]X. Pi. 2019. "China's Factories Are Struggling to Hire Enough Workers," *Bloomberg.* www.bloomberg.com/news/articles/2019-03-07/what-trade-war-china-s-factory-hub-can-t-hire-enough-workers, (accessed February 2, 2020).

> *"After phone interviews, the list of candidates is cut in half. Once references, past employment, and qualifications are verified, we might be left with one or two resumes. Since most managers want to interview at least three candidates, we need to go through 16 to 20 resumes to fill one position.*

The most difficult jobs to fill in China are those requiring high skill. This is particularly true in towns and villages where manufacturing in China is concentrated. The labor pool is small, and few people are interested in relocating to these areas. One way around the skills gap is to break up high-skilled jobs into a number of low-skilled jobs. Although "de-skilling" makes recruitment easier, getting anything done requires coordinating activities across a chain of people. People in the chain have such a narrow focus that they seldom see how tasks come together to produce value. Quality, customer service, and problem-solving suffer.

Adding to the labor efficiency problem is workforce demographics. China's *One Child Policy* was in effect from 1979 through 2015. During this period, families were permitted to have only a single child.[12] The goal was to reduce poverty by allowing economic growth to outpace population growth. From 1979 to 1998, the Chinese economy expanded by an average of 10 percent per year.[13] At the same time the Chinese birth rate fell from 2.8 births per woman to 1.6.[14] As a result, hundreds of millions of people were lifted out of poverty. Unfortunately for industry, population demographics shifted. The largest population increases have been among people at or near retirement. "In 2009, 12.2% of factory workers in China were aged 50 years or older. By 2019, that number had grown to 24.6%."[15] Employees in their late 20s through early 30s are highly

---

[12]Exceptions included twins or farmers whose firstborn child was a girl.

[13]*EveryCRSReport.com*. 2019. "China's Economic Rise: History, Trends, Challenges and Implications for the United States," www.everycrsreport.com/reports/RL33534. html, (accessed January 2, 2019).

[14]J. Kuepper. 2019. "China Changed to a Two-Child Policy in 2016," *The Balance*. www. thebalance.com/china-one-child-economy-1979075, (accessed February 19, 2020).

[15]Q. Chen. 2020. "Chinese Factory Workers Are Greying Quickly," *Inkstone*. https:// www.inkstonenews.com/business/inkstone-index-chinese-factory-workers-are-graying-quickly/article/3103329?utm_medium=partner&utm_campaign=contentex changeinkstone&utm_source=Smartnews, (accessed March 2, 2021).

sought after by employers. However, this demographic has experienced the smallest population growth.

Few job applicants are over the age of 35 because many people, by this time, have already found permanent employment. Officially, all full-time employees work under labor contracts. After an employee's first contract expires, the employer has the option of offering a second contract. After the second contract ends, if the employer wishes to retain the employee, a permanent contract must be offered.

In addition to dealing with a labor pool that has reduced on average by 0.5 percent per year from 2012 through 2019, operations managers also face the problem of underqualified applicants.[16] According to a 2013 report, 35 percent of Chinese students completing a 4-year degree lacked sufficient skills to find work in their field.[17] Prospects were even worse for vocational school graduates. The same study found that 70 percent lacked necessary skills to find work in their areas of study. Some blame the lack of skills on funding. Public spending on education in China is a mere 4 percent of GDP.[18] Others blame the education system. A heavy emphasis on memorization, test taking, and conformity tends to produce graduates lacking creativity or a lifelong love of learning.

Like most other high school students across China, she was in class by 7:00 am. After five 45-minute lectures, she ate lunch and then took the mandatory 1-hour nap in the dormitory.

Afternoon classes consisted of four more 45-minute lectures followed by dinner in the cafeteria. By 6:00 p.m. she was back in class for another

[16]W. Connett. 2019. "Understanding China's Former One Child Policy," *Investopedia.* www.investopedia.com/articles/investing/120114/understanding-chinas-one-child-policy.asp, (accessed November 15, 2019).

[17]L. Dai. 2013. "The Undergraduate Signing Rate is Only 35% which is 12% Lower than Last Year," *Beijing Evening News.* http://edu.qq.com/a/20130609/013282.htm, (accessed June 23, 2018).

[18]Z. Liu and H. Yamamoto. 2009. "Public Private Partnerships (PPP) in China: Present Conditions and Future Challenges," *Graduate School of Information Sciences Tohoku University.* www.webssa.net/files/cas_ppp.pdf, (accessed February 20, 2019).

4 hours of review. Most nights she didn't finish her homework until midnight.

All this hard work was done in preparation for the national "gaokao" college entrance exam. She tried to be optimistic but knew the odds were stacked against her. Close to 11 million students were taking a test for seven million openings.

When negotiating pay packages with new graduates, employers often find the lack of skills translates into low wages.[19] From 2003 through 2009, the average starting salary for migrant laborers grew 80 percent. At the same time, starting pay for college graduates didn't change.[20] However, unlike migrants, new graduates often expect their salaries to double in 2 to 3 years. The reason for the pay increase is simply supply and demand.

There's a large supply of small manufacturers offering low-paying jobs. New graduates take these jobs in the hope of acquiring skills necessary to land better paying jobs elsewhere. Changing jobs is so prevalent that it's not uncommon to find applicants in their mid-20s who have already worked for three or four different employers. Before making an offer, it's important to remember that Chinese labor is a fixed cost.

Employees work under contracts. Common terms are 1, 2, or 3 years. The first month of a 1-year contract (or 3 months of a 3-year contract) is the probationary period. The employer can terminate the contract at any point during this time. Once the probation period ends, the employee is guaranteed the job as specified in the labor contract for the duration of the contract. The employee has the right to refuse any work outside of what's specified in the contract. Failing to offer a contract isn't a viable option. As of 2019, if an employee works 1 year without an employment contract, the employee is automatically entered in a permanent contract until retirement.

---

[19]The exception being graduates from China's top universities. Their wage expectations are very high.

[20]A. Jacobs. 2010. "After University in China: Ant Tribes, Sea Turtles and Difficulty Finding a Job," *New York Times.* http://factsanddetails.com/china/cat13/sub82/item1719.html, (accessed February 2, 2020).

To open up the possibility of job transfers, managers typically try to use very broad language when describing what people do and where they work. To ensure wording follows local labor bureau guidelines (and is enforceable in light of local court decisions), HR managers might ask local lawyers to review contracts before presenting them for signature.

"The job description is fine. But calling people 'packers' is very restrictive. You can't require them do anything other than packing. You might want to replace the term 'packer' with 'assembly department associate.' Under this title associates can be asked to assemble products, pack boxes, or move pallets around the warehouse."

The hiring manager agreed and changed the job title. Newly hired assembly department associates were paid the same as packers. Initially, new hires complained. They were doing more work for less pay. Over time, they saw that as packer contracts came due, only those willing to sign on as assembly department associates were rehired.

Packers with permanent contracts couldn't be asked to perform the added responsibilities of assembly department associates. But they also received the lowest monthly bonuses. Most got the message and transferred to other departments.

Employees and local labor bureaus alike prefer labor contracts with narrowly defined roles and responsibilities. On the one hand, workers can't be asked to do too many things. On the other hand, operations managers need to hire more people as this keeps unemployment low. A successful HR manager is able to write employment contracts as broadly as management wants, the local labor bureau allows, and workers are willing to sign.

When presenting labor contracts for signature, HR managers are typically dealing directly with employees. The lack of collective bargaining is surprising, considering that the All-China Federation of Trade Unions (ACFTU) is the world's largest union. What's holding collective bargaining back? There simply isn't that much to negotiate. National Ministry of Labor and Social Security (MOLSS) guidelines cover the following:

1. Pensions, unemployment, medical insurance, workman's compensation, and maternity leave

2. Vocational curriculum, accreditation, and certification
3. Employment of foreign workers
4. Use of employment agencies
5. Laying off and reassigning of SOE workers.

Local labor bureau policies address the following:

1. Working conditions
2. Job safety
3. Discipline
4. Training
5. Contracts and pay

Another reason collective bargaining has been slow to take hold is the way ACFTU chapters are organized. Chapters aren't at the national, state, or even local level. Each is set up by the company. Management and labor in the company both belong to the same union. While management (and their immediate families) can't serve as union leaders, it isn't unusual for a member of the senior management team to step down in order to serve as union chairperson. Why would shop floor workers give up the chance to have one of their own speak for them as chairperson? By law, the chairperson must be a member of the Party and approved for the position by the Party. It can be the case that no shop floor associates qualify to serve.

What does the union chairperson actually do? Companies in China are required to set aside 2 percent of payroll for the benefit of employees. The chairperson is responsible for distributing these funds. Common disbursements include a free meal during the workday, annual health screenings, Family Day picnics, Sports Day competitions, and, as Figure 4.3 shows, elaborate Chinese New Year's celebrations.

For HR managers, dealing with the company union isn't normally a problem. The challenge is keeping up with changes in local labor policy. For example, within 10 days of an announcement all employers are required to be in compliance with government policy changes. Announcements can come at any time (and any number of times) during the year.

Figure 4.3 New Year's show being put on by employees

Source: Courtesy of Acco Brands.

A group of employees brought a newspaper into the HR manager's office. "It says here the minimum wage increased 5 percent last month. Why didn't our pay go up?"

"The increase doesn't apply to you. You already earn more than the new minimum wage."

"But the article says pay increases are needed to offset rising prices. This affects us too."

Half an hour later another group of employees arrived carrying the same article and making many of the same arguments. This went on for a few weeks. At the end of the year, management decided to increase wages (including their own) by the same percentage by which minimum wage increased.

It's not unusual to find companies ignoring labor laws. After all, two-thirds of Chinese workers are migrants who, by definition, are illegally working outside their *hukou* area. Workers with labor contracts are in a different situation. They have protections that make dismissing them very difficult. For example, pregnant workers, those on maternity leave, or anyone suffering a work-related injury can't be dismissed. If job cuts are large enough to be considered restructuring, operations managers need local labor bureau approval before proceeding.

After reviewing company financials, the mayor's office approved head count reductions. The first category of people cut were those within 5 years of retirement. Compensation offered was 1 month's pay for every year worked plus one additional month's pay. Monthly pay used in the calculation was average wages in the city over the past 5 years.

The second category of people cut were those with 1 year or less on their employment contracts. They also received 1 month's pay for every year worked plus an additional month's pay. Monthly pay used in this calculation was employees' existing wages.

The last category were low performers. The mayor's office agreed they could be let go but only if alternative employment could be found for them in the city.

Unlike restructuring, dismissing individual employees doesn't require local labor bureau approval. Under the *Provisions Concerning Economic Redundancy in Enterprises,* employees can be cut if they're:

- Given 30 days' notice.
- Unable to perform work as specified in the contract even after receiving additional training.
- Unwilling to accept a new job even after the original job had significantly changed or no longer exists.

Employees have the right to grieve job loss or compensation offered to the local labor bureau. Mediating individual labor disputes isn't something the local labor bureau is interested in doing. To avoid running afoul of local officials, operations managers tend to dismiss those least likely to grieve. In many cases this is part-time employees working without labor contracts or full-time employees near retirement.

Since 1997, China has run a contributory pension system. Employees contribute 8 percent of wages toward pensions. Employers contribute 16 percent of employee wages toward pensions.[21] Depending on where

---

[21]When ending work assignments in China, foreigners can apply for reimbursement of their pension contributions. Company contributions, however, aren't refunded.

companies are located, social security benefits such as pensions, medical, unemployment insurance, and housing are managed either by the city or by provincial government. In theory, the total amount invested in an employee's pension plan (plus interest) is divided by 139 to calculate the associate's annual benefit in perpetuity. In reality, the amount could be much less. A 2013 China Pension Report found the pension system was almost 3 trillion RMB underfunded.[22] Potential reasons for the shortfall include:

- Government workers draw pensions but don't contribute to them.
- Pensions are poorly administrated.

How solvent a soon-to-be retired worker perceives the local pension scheme is plays a big part in whether or not to accept early retirement. The other issue is how HR managers calculate contract buyout amounts.

The typical buyout for anyone under contract is 1 month's pay for every year worked plus an additional month's pay. Employees expect monthly pay in this calculation to be their pay at the time of separation. However, the legal requirement is average monthly pay in the city over all years worked. This amount can be far less than what employees are willing to accept when they've been paid well above average city wages.

In light of these difficulties, managers might pursue voluntary layoffs in place of voluntary retirements. As with any change in employment contracts, employees and employers must agree on terms. Common layoff terms include the following:

- Continuation of monthly pay as a percentage of the local city average wage
- Continuation of benefits
- New employees can't be hired until all laid-off workers have been offered their jobs back.

---

[22]Y. Wang. 2013. "China's Pension System Gets More Troubled," *Forbes*. www.forbes.com/sites/ywang/2013/12/12/chinas-pension-system-gets-more-troubled/, (accessed February 12, 2017).

- If laid-off workers accept employment elsewhere, layoff payments end.[23]

If an employee refuses the proposed layoff package and the employer still wishes to proceed, the employee can grieve to the local labor bureau. The local labor bureau acts as arbitrator, and its decision is final.

To avoid the problem of labor working under fixed contracts, employers have traditionally relied on part-time and contingent labor. Part-time employees are not required to have contracts. They can be dismissed anytime, and severance pay isn't required. But they can work only 4 hours a day. Working hours per week cannot exceed 24 hours. Contingent workers can work full time, and, like part-time workers, they don't have labor contracts with the companies where they work. They do, however, have contracts with agencies that place them in companies. Managers at these companies can bring contingents on and move them out as needed. By 2013, contingents made up close to 20 percent of China's workforce. Such a high dependence on contingent labor clearly violated the spirit of China's Labor Contract Law. Subsequent amendments to the law have made it difficult for companies to employ contingents for anything other than temporary assignments not exceeding 1 year. In 2020, Apple was accused of ignoring the 10 percent limit on the proportion of temporary workers at its suppliers out of fear that costs would rise and product launches would be delayed.[24]

In the continuing search for low-cost flexible labor, some employers have turned to vocational schools. In these arrangements, companies sign labor contracts with schools. Schools provide student labor. Each student can work up to 40 hours per week in an area related to their major, with overtime not to exceed 8 hours per week. Employers sometimes ignore student labor restrictions. For example, in 2020, Apple suspended

---

[23]Employers know when laid-off workers find full-time jobs because new employers request social security paperwork.

[24]K. Dully. 2020. "Former Apple Employees Have Accused the Company of Turning a Blind Eye to Suppliers That Were Violating Chinese Labor Laws," *Insider.* https://www.businessinsider.com/former-apple-employees-apple-ignored-suppliers-violated-china-labor-laws-2020-12, (accessed February 3, 2021).

business with Pegatron, its second-largest Chinese iPhone manufacturer, for misclassifying students in order to assign them night shift work and additional overtime. Without the protection of an employment contract, it could be the case that students are:

- Paid less than the city minimum wage
- Not entitled to benefits
- Dismissed as needed

A problem with employing students is that many leave after the school year ends. To retain key talent, companies might offer to pay tuition if students (or their parents) sign promissory notes. It isn't unusual for promissory terms to require repayment of education expenses if students leave employment within 2 to 3 years of graduation. Although repayment costs are high for students, they're small for prospective employers.

It's common practice when recruiting talent from other companies to pay off outstanding promissory notes. It's also common practice to offer contract signing bonuses worth 1 to 2 months' salary. Besides paying to onboard talent, managers can find that to retain even mediocre employees they need to offer three to 6 percent annual wage increases. In addition, it's not unusual for employees to expect 20 to 30 percent pay-for-performance monthly bonuses.

Workers in the production cell routinely complained that the highest bonuses always went to the supervisor's friends. When asked what it took to be his friend, most agreed it was some combination of working hard, doing what you're told, learning new skills, and socializing with him. One worker explained, "My monthly bonus is usually 25 percent. Even if I was offered a pay increase to work in another department, I wouldn't go. My new boss probably has enough friends. I'd never get a good bonus and end up making less than I do now."

With so much compensation tied to performance, it's common for factory workers to quit when orders decrease.

The factory was running at 30 percent of capacity. Without much to do, workers complained that the bonus plan never paid out. Some started leaving.

Management was worried that if too many workers left, the plant wouldn't be able to meet customer demand when orders picked up. The bonus plan was adjusted. It paid out based on achieving scrap targets, keeping work areas clean, and taking part in cross-training. Most operators stayed.

Within 6 months orders increased. Unexpectedly, operators started quitting again.

When asked why, a common answer was, "Under the old pay plan we always received our monthly bonuses. We didn't need to do too much. Now, we have to work twice as hard for the same pay."

Factory output in China typically spikes in the months leading up to Chinese Spring Festival (also known as Lunar New Year). The reasons are culture and pay. During the festival approximately 400 million people will be traveling back to their hometowns. Rail, road, and air congestion (as shown in Figure 4.4) force many employees to leave work before the holiday begins and return after it ends. As a result, companies rush to fill orders (or build inventory) before their workforce departs.

Figure 4.4 Spring Festival travel congestion

Source: Courtesy of Xubiao Wu.

Spring Festival was approaching. The department manager knew most of his staff would be gone for at least a week. Those with family living farther away would be gone longer. He expected that some workers, after receiving their New Year's bonus, would never return. Other departments faced similar issues.

The general manager decided to close the factory for a month. While the decision hurt sales, it made production planning easier for the remainder of the year. Everyone used up their paid vacation at the same time.

One way companies ensure employees don't quit in the busy months leading up to Spring Festival is paying wages on a 13-month year. For example, suppose a local manager earns 72,000 RMB per year. This works out to 6,000 RMB/month (i.e., 72,000/12). Under a 13-month pay plan, 500 RMB (i.e., 1/12 of the 6,000/month) is held back each pay period. In the 13th month the employee receives monthly pay of 5,500 RMB plus the accumulated 13th month pay of 6,000 RMB (i.e., 12 × 500 RMB). In addition to receiving a 13th month's salary during Spring Festival, employees expect an annual bonus. Most, if not all, of this bonus will be tax free.

For one pay period per year, the Chinese tax bureau divides total bonus compensation by 12 to calculate taxable income. In the example cited, suppose that, in addition to the 6,000 RMB 13th month pay, the employee receives a 10,000 RMB bonus. Of the 16,000 RMB bonus only 1,333 RMB (i.e., 16,000/12) is taxable. Per Table 4.1, the first 1,500 RMB of income earned in a month is taxed at 3 percent.[25]

The employee in the example would pay only 40 RMB tax on a 16,000 RMB bonus. This works out to roughly one-third of annual take-home pay earned in 1 month. It's common for employees in China to earn most of their annual compensation in 1 month. It could be the case that migrant workers are paid only once a year.

Managing lump-sum cash payments also requires that managers understand workers' compensation. It's common to see signs and banners in factories and, as Figure 4.5 shows, on street corners bearing slogans relating to hard work, health, safety, and so forth.

---

[25] *World-wide tax.com.* 2017. "China Tax and Tax Laws," www.worldwide-tax.com/china/china_tax.asp, (accessed May 18, 2018).

Table 4.1 Income tax by salary level, 2017

Tax (%)	Income/month (RMB)
45	80,001+
35	55,001–80,000
39	35,001–55,000
25	9,001–35,000
29	4,501–9,000
10	1,501–4,500
3	1–1,500

Figure 4.5 Signs promoting patriotism, democracy, prosperity, civilization, harmony, equality, justice, law, devotion to work, kindness, integrity

Source: Courtesy of Xubiao Wu.

The reality is that workplace injuries are a very large problem in China—so large that in 2012 China recorded 1 million work-related injuries and 80,000 deaths.[26] By 2018 the number of work-related accidents

---

[26]*China Labour Bulletin*. 2012. "An Introduction to China's Work-Related Injury Compensation System," www.clb.org.hk/en/content/introduction-chinas-work-related-injury-compensation-system (May 17, 2018).

and deaths fell by 95 percent and 56 percent, respectively.[27] A big reason for the drop is clearer definitions and enforcement of company liability.

For an injury to be considered work related, it must be diagnosed by an accredited physician at a state-run hospital. Besides confirming injury, the *Work-Related Injury Insurance Regulations Manual* stipulates the following requirements:

- The worker has a valid employment contract.
- The employer has a valid business license to conduct the type of work being done.
- The injury is a direct result of working conditions.
- The injury occurs in preparation for, during, or at the conclusion of work, a business trip, or an assignment outside of work.
- The injury is sustained when protecting public interests.
- A prior military injury is reinjured.

By the above definitions, injuries occurring on the way to or from work are work related. In 2019 a quarter of a million people in China died in traffic accidents, making road accidents the main cause of death for people aged 15 to 45 years.[28] Liability and the high probability of injury explain why many operations in China provide bus transport for employees.

A number of employees rode electric scooters to work. They were cheap and fast, and the plant provided free charging stations.

Since scooters didn't require licenses, many riders ignored traffic rules. One evening, while weaving in and out of traffic on his way home from work, an employee crashed. His employer ended up paying the hospital bill. Not long after, free charging points were removed and bus services were provided.

---

[27] *China Labour Bulletin*. 2019. "Work Accidents and Deaths in China Fall But Familiar Failings Remain," https://clb.org.hk/content/work-accidents-and-deaths-china-fall-familiar-failings-remain, (accessed February 2, 2020).

[28] *China Labour Bulletin*. 2019. "Work Accidents and Deaths in China Fall But Familiar Failings Remain," https://clb.org.hk/content/work-accidents-and-deaths-china-fall-familiar-failings-remain, (accessed February 2, 2020). *International Driving Authority*. 2019. "Chinese Traffic Rules," https://idaoffice.org/posts/chinese-traffi%25d1%2581-rules/, (accessed February 10, 2020).

Assuming an injury claim can be made, the next steps are assessing degree of disability and compensation owed. Severity is graded one through 10 by the *Standard for Determining the Seriousness of Work-related Injuries and Occupational Diseases.* Compensation is also by grade according to the *Social Insurance Law and Law on the Prevention and Treatment of Occupational Diseases.*

Disability payments typically start with a lump sum. The amount can vary from 27 months' pay (for the most serious Grade 1 injuries) to 7 months' pay (for a Grade 10 injury). A month's pay in this calculation is based on the employee's average pay over the previous year. The National Worker Injury Insurance Fund (which employees must pay into every month) covers this cost.

The injured employee may also qualify for monthly disability payments. The amount can be as high as 90 percent of the employee's salary at the time of injury (for a Grade 1 injury) to 60 percent (for a Grade 6 injury). In the case of Grade 1 through 4 injuries, payments are made out of the Worker Injury Insurance Fund. Grade 5 through 6 injuries are paid by employers.

If long-term nursing care is needed, payments are made out of the Worker Injury Insurance Fund. Depending on injury grade, payments can be anywhere from 50 to 30 percent of the average local wage where the employee works.

If an injured employee no longer wishes to continue working (or the employer wishes to end the contract), the employee is eligible for two lump-sum payments. One is a medical subsidy; the other is a disability payment. Depending on injury grade, the medical subsidy can be anywhere from four to 14 percent of the average wage in the local area. This is paid out of the Worker Injury Insurance Fund. The disability payment varies from six to 60 percent of the local average wage and is paid by the employer. Given the wide range of disability payments, amounts, calculations, and responsibilities, disagreements and misunderstandings are common.

Negotiations between managers and injured workers can be very complicated. The same can be said for negotiations involving pay, bonuses, voluntary labor reductions, and involuntary ones. Generally speaking, it's best to handle problems internally. The local labor bureau has little interest in arbitrating disputes. A good working relationship with the local labor bureau is key because the bureau ultimately decides what labor laws say and whether employers are in compliance.

CHAPTER 5

Management

As of 2018 the average minimum wage in China was $180 per month in small tier 4 cities. It was $330 per month in large tier 1 cities.[1] Although these amounts are three to six times lower than the U.S. minimum wage, Chinese minimum wages have increased 64 percent from 2011 to 2018.[2] A key challenge in managing operations in China is doing more with fewer people.

[Pete is an expatriate project manager working in China. He's having a lot of problems with the purchasing department. To him buyers seem to lack even the most basic skills. He's decided to share his frustrations with the plant manager.]

"Almost 70 percent of our manufacturing costs are in purchased parts. Buying is critical if we're going to be successful."

"I agree. That's why we have a strong purchasing manager."

"The manager is strong. But he needs to have a stronger team. Buyers don't do anything without his approval."

"They're inexperienced. He wants to make sure they don't make mistakes."

"He should hire more experienced people."

---

[1] A. Koty. 2018. "Guangdong's Minimum Wages to Increase July 1," *Dezan, Shira and Associates.* www.china-briefing.com/news/guangdongs-minimum-wages-rise-july-1/, (accessed May 13, 2019).

[2] S. Yan. 2017. "'Made in China' Isn't So Cheap Anymore, and that Could Spell Headache for Beijing," *CNBC Markets.* www.cnbc.com/2017/02/27/chinese-wages-rise-made-in-china-isnt-so-cheap-anymore.html, (accessed September 12, 2018).

"Experienced buyers are in short supply. Even if he could find them, I'm sure their salary demands would be beyond what we pay. Anyway, bringing in people like that can create conflict."

"How can skill create conflict?"

"They wouldn't want to work as entry-level buyers for very long. Their hard work and dedication would eventually outshine their manager. To rein in potential challengers he might start complaining about their work. Some people would side with the manager. Others would see buyers as being unfairly treated. Either way, people would lose focus. Customer service would suffer. Best to avoid all the drama and hire people who fit in."

In the example cited, Pete and the plant manager clearly have different opinions about improving efficiency. If Pete's going to be successful working in China, he needs to be able to see situations from a Chinese perspective. An effective way to do this is to read Chinese history. For example, at the start of the Ming Dynasty (1368 to 1644), Emperor Hongwu centralized all power under himself. With great power came great suspicion. He viewed court eunuchs, who had traditionally served as intermediaries between the emperor and his court, with suspicion. To mitigate their influence, he made teaching them to read illegal. Had Pete been familiar with the story of Emperor Hongwu, the purchasing manager's decision to surround himself with low-skilled staff would have made more sense. In both instances leaders were willing to forego efficiency for the sake of individual power.

Reading over 4,000 years of Chinese history to gain management insight is a daunting task. It doesn't help that most books go into a level of detail well beyond what businesspeople need to know. In this chapter, present-day management practices are explained by placing them in a historical context.

From kings to emperors, regents, warlords, rebels, generals, presidents, and so on, China has experienced them all. Successive generations of Chinese have come to accept that those in power share at least one thing in common—the desire to stay in power. During the Han Dynasty (206 BC to 220 AD), leaders were able to stay in power by replacing local kings with loyal family members. Today, owners of small- to medium-sized factories routinely staff key positions with family members.

[While touring the factory, Jim was introduced to the owner's wife, Ms. Zhang].

"Nice to meet you. Do you work here?"

"Yes. I'm the purchasing manager."

"That's a difficult job."

"It sure is. We assemble a lot of purchased parts. I make sure we're getting the best prices."

"Do you negotiate everything yourself?"

"I have a staff. But they don't get involved in price negotiations."

"Why?"

"They don't have enough experience. Most of them have only been in the department for two or three years."

"That's too bad?"

"It's ok. If they stay any longer they might start taking advantage."

When it's not possible to recruit a relative or close friend, hometown can play an important role. A manager raised in the South might surround him or herself with direct reports from the South. A manager from the North might do the same with fellow Northerners. Why? For 750 years spanning the Six Dynasties (220 to 589 AD), Five Dynasties (907 to 960 AD), and Song Dynasty (960 to 1289 AD), China was divided north and south of the Yangtze River, as shown in Figure 5.1. Distinct North and South cultures emerged, which remain in place today.

Whether managers are from the North or South, one of their first acts will likely be removing potential challengers.

Over the course of 4 months, the new general manager reassigned every member of the senior management team. When asked why, he explained, "Those people were loyal to the previous manager. Some undoubtedly felt they should have been offered my job. A few probably deserved it. There was no way any of them were going to accept me. I needed to get rid of them and put in my people."

Many of his people had little to no experience in the departments they were now managing. The general manager didn't seem concerned. "The new managers are clever and can quickly figure out what needs to be done. It's actually better that they don't know too much. Otherwise, they'd have their own agendas and start questioning my decisions. Better to promote people who know they have their jobs because I favor them. They'll protect me in order to protect themselves."

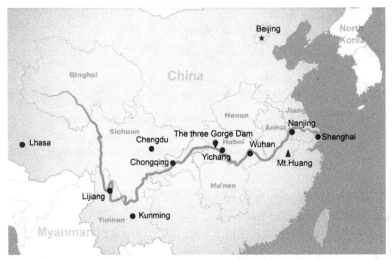

Figure 5.1   The Yangtze River divides China geographically and culturally

Source: Courtesy of www.chinahighlights.com.

Clearing out rivals is nothing new. To varying degrees Emperor Qin (221 to 208 BC), Emperor Wen (541 to 604 AD), Emperor Hongwu (1328 to 1398), and Chairman Mao Zedong (1893 to 1976) were all able to unify China by redistributing wealth and power in exchange for loyalty. Whose loyalty will department managers and work stream leaders likely seek out? Could it be critical thinkers passionate about finding better ways to do things? Probably not. These people tend to upset the balance of power.

Chinese history is full of stories about rebels bringing down empires. Ji Fa ended the Shang Dynasty (1700 to 1045 BC), Ying Zhen ended the Zhou Dynasty (1045 to 256 BC), Liu Bang ended the Qin Dynasty (221 to 208 BC), Cao Cao ended the Han Dynasty (206 BC to 220 AD), Chu Yuan Chang ended the Yuan Dynasty (1279 to 1368), and Li Zicheng ended the Ming Dynasty (1368 to 1644).

The project was behind schedule. The project manager blamed an engineer who was ignoring assignments. When discussing the problem with her, the project manager became upset and slammed his hand on her desk.

The engineer complained to HR. HR agreed that the project manager had acted inappropriately.

The project manager was required to sign a letter of apology. The letter explained how stress brought on by working outside established reporting channels had caused him to lose control. The letter was posted at the company entrance for all to see.

Local managers will typically want direct reports who accept the five tenets of Confucius thought. These are:

- Loyalty to leader
- Getting by with what you have
- Protecting family name
- Following socially acceptable behavior
- Having faith in the system.

Like the Qin Dynasty legalists of old, these employees attach great importance to actions benefiting their leader. And, in keeping with Taoist thought, they don't complain too loudly. They accept that poor management decisions happen because good and bad happen in balance. Best to follow the rules and assimilate.

[One of the machines needed a screw. The expatriate project manager went to the warehouse to ask the attendant for one.]

"You'll need to fill out a slip of paper."

"Ok. Here you go."

"This needs to be approved by a manager."

"I am a manager."

"Please wait."

"Why?"

"I need to ask my manager what to do."

"What's the problem?"

"The requisition paper has a space for requestor and manager signatures. The same name can't be on both lines."

[40 minutes pass]

"You'll have to fill out the paper and ask the plant manager for approval."

"Why?"

"He's your manager."

"This screw probably costs less than 1 jiao.[1] Do you really want me to bother the plant manager with a 1 jiao requisition order?"

"Please wait. I have to ask my manager."

[Another 40 minutes pass. A repairman shows up.]

"The repairman will fill out the requisition, and you can approve it."

---

[1]One jiao is worth slightly more than a U.S. penny.

Bureaucracy is an integral part of Chinese organizations. It could be argued that this has been so since the Han (from which more than 90 percent of mainland Chinese are ethnically descended) came to power in 206 BC. Today, it isn't unusual for managers to install just enough lines of reporting in organizations to put down potential challengers while at the same time insulating themselves from blame should anything go wrong. The result is a culture immersed in top-down decision making.

The senior management team met daily. They discussed budgets, projects, and capital spending.

They also made a lot of day-to-day decisions such as how best to schedule production cells or which machines to repair.

Many supervisors and department managers were a lot closer to these daily issues. Yet they contributed very little to the conversations. When asked if they would like to be more involved, most weren't interested. "In every decision there are winners and losers. Why risk making a mistake and upsetting powerful people? Better to just listen to my leader and be rewarded for doing what I'm told."

Decision making can easily become less about problem-solving than about protecting one's position in the hierarchy. After all, those who've put problem-solving before self-preservation haven't fared very well throughout Chinese history.

- The Northern Song Empire (960 to 1289) was smaller and poorer than the previous Tang Empire (618 to 907). Any hope of reestablishing lucrative Silk Road trade routes hinged on defeating Jurchen tribes in Central Asia. Unfortunately, a war of conquest soon turned into one of survival. Jurchen forces overran the Song and set up their own empire.
- Following defeats at the hands of the British (1839 to 1842) and Japanese (1894 to 1895), Emperor Guangxu (1871 to 1908) was convinced China needed to modernize. During the Hundred Days' Reform, he introduced capitalism and a constitutional monarchy. The ruling elites didn't care much for these changes, and Emperor Guangxu was soon deposed in a coup.
- After one of the worst man-made famines in human history (1958 to 1962), some in the government were calling for an interim period of capitalism (to create wealth), followed by a longer period of socialism (to redistribute wealth). The Red Guard was deployed to purge society of such counterrevolutions.

It can be the case that local managers equate success not so much with solving problems as with strengthening their positions in organizations.

The plant manager wanted to reduce inventory without sacrificing capacity. That meant running smaller batch sizes with faster machine tooling changes.

A young engineer had an idea how to do this. He knew that if he spoke directly with senior management they'd likely ignore him. Worse yet, if they did listen, more experienced people in his department would be blamed for not coming up with the solution. They would make sure his idea failed.

He decided to tell his manager about his idea. But he didn't take credit for it. He said the idea was based on discussions he had had with senior engineers in the department.

> *The engineering manager liked his idea. He thanked the senior engineers for coaching the less experienced engineer.*
>
> *The idea worked. So did his approach. He solved the problem, made the higher-ups look good, and strengthened ties with influential coworkers.*

A focus on self-preservation can lead to high levels of risk avoidance.

> *A team of Lean Manufacturing specialists from the United States arrived in China to teach problem-solving. They led daily training sessions with local supervisors, engineers, and technicians. Attendees dutifully took notes and praised their instructors. By the end of the week, meeting room walls were covered with Gant charts, decision trees, fishbone diagrams, Pareto charts, and so on.*
>
> *Monday morning of the following week, trainers and trainees gathered at a machine cell to put theory into practice. Eight hours later, trainers left the shop confused and dejected. One trainer, while boarding the company bus back to the hotel, was overheard muttering, "No one could find a problem. They wouldn't even look."*
>
> *The next day everyone met in the conference room to discuss what had happened on Monday. One trainee explained, "My job is buying consumables. I know how much every production cell needs. If productivity improves, I won't know how much to order. Everyone will blame me." Another person chimed in, "We work in that cell. Our monthly bonuses are based on schedule accomplishment. If productivity improves, we'll be asked to make more for the same pay." A shift supervisor eventually came forward and admitted, "I was hoping no one would come up with anything. If someone did, my boss would hold me accountable for implementing it. I'm already too busy."*

Trainers in the example cited didn't fail to teach. They failed to appreciate that throughout China's feudal, imperial, and socialist histories what one does is far less important than for whom it is done.

> *A Lean Manufacturing trainer replied, "If no one intended to implement process improvements, what was the point of training?"*
>
> *The room erupted in conversation. Trainees talked over each other for the next 20 minutes. After the room quieted down, one person suggested, "Why don't you give us a test?"*

> *"Why?"*
>
> *"It will show your boss how well you trained us, and our boss will know that we paid attention. Everyone wins." Trainees nodded their heads in agreement. Trainers shook theirs in disbelief.*

Although bureaucracies tend to permeate every level of Chinese operations, they are functional only when a single, strong leader is present. For example, during the Warring States and Five Dynasties periods, this wasn't the case. China experienced nearly 300 years of internal conflict. Modern-day operations can also experience competing factions when a strong leader is absent.

> *The general manager never stopped making decisions. All day long he fielded questions from managers in accounting, HR, scheduling, engineering, and production. No one could possibly have known the answers to all their questions.*
>
> *When asked if this worried him, the plant manager laughed. "Most of the time they already know what to do. They just ask me to show how hard they're working and to make sure if anything goes wrong I won't blame them. Even if I make a few wrong decisions, they'll make things work somehow."*
>
> *"What if they can't?"*
>
> *"My informants will tell me."*
>
> *Who?"*
>
> *"People I know at lower levels in the company. They tell me what's really happening. Every manager has them. It's how we stay one step ahead."*

Like nineteenth century warlords, midlevel managers might seek to protect their interest by forming cliques with other managers. Cliques can cause significant disruptions as they vie for power. One way operations managers can protect against this is keeping influential people close. This practice stretches back to the Zhou Dynasty (1045 to 256 BC). Zhou leaders were able to expand their empire not by getting rid of rival chiefs but by giving them just as much power as was in their best interest to remain loyal.

The engineering manager was asked to lead a process improvement team. Within 4 months his team boosted productivity 30 percent.

Two months later the plant started receiving customer complaints. The quality manager blamed the new process. The engineering manager produced data showing the process was capable.

Over the next few weeks, finished product inspectors continued to find nonconforming parts. The general manager needed to do something. He decided to reinstate the old process.

After the change, inspectors were still finding nonconforming parts. A production supervisor going through a batch of bad parts noticed that they were all made on the third shift.

He knew there were some new operators on the third shift. Did their work assignments overlap with areas where bad parts were made? A quick look at their training records would tell him if this was possible.

He couldn't find their training reports. This was impossible. Their training ended 7 weeks ago. He told the production manager what he discovered.

The production manager and HR manager pieced together what had happened. The previous training coordinator quit. Her leaving coincided with the hiring of these operators. For the duration of their training period no one trained them. Not long after, a new supervisor was hired on the third shift. He assumed the previous supervisor had approved their training reports. He assigned them to work in the cells that ended up making the bad parts.

With the problem solved, the general manager was free to put the more productive process back in place. He didn't. When asked why, he explained,

> *Productivity gains were needed. But I had a bigger opportunity. The production and HR managers had more experience than me. I needed their full support. I explained to them the process change would be blamed for the training oversight. Their failures would remain secret.*

From that point onward, the production and HR managers were his strongest supporters.

When outcomes don't determine right and wrong, what does? In Chinese organizations "right" is doing what leaders say.

> *The workshop manager along with his supervisors and technicians created a new machine layout. They worked with Engineering to make drawings, Facilities to move equipment, and Maintenance to install piping and wires.*
>
> *A week later, the general manager was walking through the workshop. He had a new machine layout idea. The next day Maintenance had the machines disconnected, and Facilities was already digging new foundations.*

Amid all the bureaucracy and politics, radical change in Chinese organizations is surprisingly easy. It happens whenever leaders with a suitable amount of influence call for it. More often than not, foreign technicians and project managers working in China lack this influence.

> *"These machines are no good. They can't hold product tolerances, and they're constantly breaking down."*
>
> *"True. But, they're cheap and we know how to fix them."*
>
> *"If we had better machines, we could be more productive."*
>
> *"True. But, in China competing on machine productivity is difficult. Everyone has essentially the same machines."*
>
> *"We can work with machine builders to upgrade our equipment."*
>
> *"True. But, many machine builders are state run. They can sell everything they make. Why would they design something new for us?"*
>
> *"We can work with smaller builders who need orders."*
>
> *"True. But many of them copy machines. They don't fully understand what they're making, much less how to improve it."*
>
> *"We could import machines."*
>
> *"True. But how would we maintain them?"*
>
> *"Many foreign machine builders have technical support offices in China."*
>
> *"True. But, the problem isn't technical service; it's the cost of service and imported parts."*
>
> *"What do you suggest?"*
>
> *"I'm not the technical expert. You are."*

Even if foreign approaches are shown to have merit, local managers might reject them. Part of the reason could be lingering doubts that foreigners have Chinese interests at heart. This is understandable considering that Eurasians (440 to 589), Jurchens (1127 to 1211), Mongols (1211 to 1368), Manchus (1644 to 1911), Germans (1881 to 1914), Japanese (1931 to 1945), and English (1898 to 1997) forces all occupied parts of China. The inability to understand how Chinese history continues to shape modern-day management decisions will, more often than not, result in well-intentioned plans falling flat.

The project manager was responsible for introducing more complex products into the factory. In his opinion, past efforts failed because operators needed more training. He designed and implemented a new training program. Unfortunately, every trained operator quit within 1 year for higher paying jobs elsewhere.

To reduce employee turnover, the project manager worked with HR to design a new pay plan. Over the next 6 months, new job descriptions were written and pay grades established. After rolling out the new pay package, there was still no improvement in employee retention.

Not long afterward, efforts to deploy more complex products into the factory ended. The project manager was reassigned.

The project manager failed. But he wasn't wrong. Better-trained employees were needed to manufacture more complex products. And better pay was needed to retain highly skilled workers.

The project manager failed because he didn't understand the bonus system. Bonus pay was a substantial part of employee compensation. The highest bonuses always went to postproduction inspections. Why? Supervisors determined bonuses. Many of them had spouses or partners working as postproduction inspectors.

CHAPTER 6

Sourcing

On the surface, sourcing in China operates no differently than in most other countries. Common steps include the following:

1. Issuing a request for quotation (RFQ).
2. If accepted, requesting production part samples (PPAP).
3. If samples are approved, preparing purchase orders (PO).
4. Following up with vendors on product quality and delivery.

What makes sourcing in China unique is how these tasks are managed. For example, Chinese manufacturers typically won't accept letter of credit (L/C) payment terms. The perception is that L/Cs carry more cost and risk for manufacturers. After all, manufacturers are usually responsible for bank advisory charges, payment charges, discrepancy charges, bank reimbursement charges, and communication charges. In China, these fees typically run anywhere from 0.75 to 1.5 percent of PO value.

In place of L/Cs, Chinese manufacturers prefer to receive 20 to 30 percent payment before work begins and the balance on shipment. This is especially true when dealing with very small companies, which often lack sufficient funds (or credit) to start work without prepayment. The risk to buyers is that after making prepayment, vendors are never able to meet quality or delivery terms. This is a particular problem when importing Chinese parts, because banking regulations make U.S. dollar cash refunds nearly impossible.

Another sourcing risk is knowing who's actually making the goods. In China, a distinction is made between traders and manufacturers. Manufacturers make products; traders sell products made by others. By law, manufacturers can't trade and traders can't manufacture.[1] In practice, the line between the two types of businesses can be blurred. For example,

---

[1] Joint ventures (JVs) are an exception. They can import and sell products manufactured by their parent company.

depending on local rules, buying finished goods, performing inspection, and repackaging qualify as manufacturing. Likewise, some manufacturers, like those shown in Figure 6.1, don't actually own factories. They move in and out of rented space.

Figure 6.1 Typical rented factory space

Source: Courtesy of Wu Xubiao.

[Two workers were taking down company signs.]
  "Are we getting new signs?"
  "No. We're just changing these for a while."
  "You mean we have to do this again?"
  "One of our distributors is having a factory tour. When their foreign customers come through, they like us to change the signs."
  "Why?"
  "It makes their customers think this is their factory."

Traders can sometimes have lower prices than manufacturers. This tends to happen when parties in supply chains:

- Lack proper registrations, licenses or land use permits
- Illegally employ migrants or use contingent labor in full-time positions
- Illegally occupy facilities not built to health, safety, or environmental codes
- Purchase counterfeit materials

[Delivery was late. This was the third time in the past 2 months. The purchasing manager asks his buyer and the expat project manager to find out what was happening.]

"Do you know this supplier?"

"No. I just picked up this account after the previous buyer quit"

"How far away is the factory?"

"It's close. We could be there in 20 minutes."

"Let's go"

[Upon their arrival, it was clear that the factory wasn't what they expected.]

"What's this place? It's huge."

"This isn't one factory. It's one building housing many factories."

"So our supplier is renting factory space?"

"It appears so. I'll call them to find out which is their unit."

[During the phone conversation it became clear that the supplier was no longer at this address.]

"We should go. Three months ago our supplier moved."

"Where are they now?"

"Very far from here. I think they've subcontracted manufacturing of our parts to another supplier."

Traders perform a delicate balancing act. On the one hand, they want customers to believe prices are fair, orders will be filled on time, and they have the ability to manage quality. On the other hand, they want their Chinese suppliers to believe markups are reasonable, lead times are attainable, quality is doable, and work being done to provide quotes will turn into orders.

Traders know that if customers figure out who's actually making their goods, they'll approach manufacturers directly for a better price. If manufacturers figure out who's actually using their products, they'll sell to them directly at a better price. Trading depends on keeping buyers and sellers in the dark. Because of this lack of transparency, traders should be avoided when:

1. Product designs aren't finalized.
2. Tolerances are tighter than Chinese national standards.
3. Process development is needed.
4. Drawings contain proprietary information.

There's also financial risk when dealing with traders. A trader's registered capital could be as low as a few thousand dollars. When faced with a quality or delivery problem, buyers might find traders don't have enough money to provide a refund.

Whenever purchasing Chinese-made parts, buyers may find quite a few vendors have no interest in providing quotes. For example, processing trade enterprises (PTEs) import raw materials, process them, then reexport finished goods. PTEs can import items duty free so long as all finished goods that they manufacture are exported. This explains why:

- Many Chinese manufacturers with export licenses export 100 percent of their production.
- Many made-in-China products are not actually available in China.

When potential vendors provide quotes, buyers should confirm they're dealing with actual companies. All registered companies in China have 15-digit registration numbers. These numbers should be included in RFQs and checked with the local Bureau of Industry and Commerce (BIC). It isn't unusual to find vendors aren't registered or that they're registered but not to make goods described in RFQs.

All Chinese businesses are required to have a business license. Licenses list activities they are authorized to perform. If a vendor is providing goods or services not listed in its business license, the company is operating illegally. It could be shut down and its assets confiscated at any time.

In addition, buyers have no right to warranty claims against vendors who lack necessary licenses.

Another risk to buyers is that vendors lack sufficient capital to cover POs. When dealing with new, potential vendors, it's advisable to run a business credit report. The report provides:

- Income statement analysis
- Balance sheet analysis
- Credit assessment
- Litigation review
- Import & Export review

To attract buyers, vendors might offer a 10 percent lower price if an official Chinese receipt (or *fapiao,* as shown in Figure 6.2) isn't provided. These vendors are hiding taxable income. It may also be the case that they're not properly registered because local tax authority can only issue prenumbered forms necessary to print official invoices and *fapiaos* to registered companies. Chinese accountants need official invoices and *fapiaos* to claim business expenses.

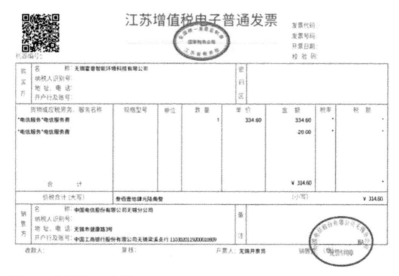

Figure 6.2 Typical Chinese fapiao

Source: Courtesy of Xubia Wu.

Besides validating sources from whom purchases are being made, buyers also need to validate the goods themselves. It is estimated that in 2016 mainland China and Hong Kong accounted for 86 percent of the world's $397-billion market in counterfeit goods.[2] These counterfeit goods make their way around the world largely through online purchases. With sales of $54 billion in 2019, Alibaba is China's largest e-commerce company. Seemingly anything buyers could ever want can be purchased on Alibaba. Unfortunately, the Office of the United States Trade Representative has placed Alibaba on its list of the world's most notorious markets for counterfeit goods.[3]

Even if purchased items aren't counterfeit, that doesn't mean they're of good quality. In 2007, Mattel recalled nearly 800,000 toys made in China for possibly containing lead paint.[4] That same year, stories circulated that a Chinese-made toothpaste was found to contain antifreeze. Not long after, a Chinese manufacturer was accused of mixing a chemical found in fertilizer with its baby formula to give the appearance of a higher protein content. In 2015 Chinese-made flooring at Lumber Liquidator was accused of failing to meet US Health and Safety limits for formaldehyde. These stories aren't isolated instances of quality failure. A 2011 report entitled "Consumer Perceptions of Product Quality: Made in China" found that the average rating for Chinese-made products fell somewhere between "I feel cheated" to "poor value."[5] As bad as the 2011 ratings were, they were actually lower than those recorded by the same study in 2004.

How is it that Chinese vendors are able to provide so many products yet are seemingly confused by the basics of quality control? They're not.

---

[2]L. Chen, et al. 2018. "8 Ways Brands Can Fight Counterfeits in China," *Harvard Business Review*. https://hbr.org/2018/05/8-ways-brands-can-fight-counterfeits-in-china, (accessed January 16, 2020).

[3]C. Li. 2016. "Alibaba Faces Growing Pressure Over Counterfeit Goods," *New York Times*. www.nytimes.com/2016/12/22/business/alibaba-ustr-taobao-counterfeit.html, (accessed August 8, 2018).

[4]*Wharton University of Pennsylvania*. 2012. "China's Manufacturers and the Quality Control Conundrum," http://knowledge.wharton.upenn.edu/article/chinas-manufacturers-and-the-quality-control-conundrum/, (accessed August 17, 2018).

[5]M. Schniederjans, Q. Cao, D. Schniederjans, and V. Gu. 2011. "Consumer Perceptions of Product Quality Revisited: Made in China," *Quality Management Journal* 18, no. 3, pp. 52–68.

In order to win orders, it's not uncommon for manufacturers to initially provide high-quality products at low or no margin. The expectation is that over time local engineers can figure out ways to cut cost. One way to cut cost is by reducing quality. The reduction is effected slow enough that performance issues aren't immediately noticeable. By the time problems are apparent, buyers have no alternative suppliers. With the balance of power shifted to vendors, they can demand price increases to solve quality issues.

To mitigate quality risk, it's common for buyers to require that products carry the China Compulsory Certificate (CCC) mark. CCC certification was introduced in 2002. It primarily covers machinery and electronics. Products requiring certification must carry the CCC mark to be imported, sold, or used in China. The mark indicates that

- A CNCA-designated test laboratory tested product samples.
- Factories were inspected and will be reinspected every 12 through 18 months.

Buyers may also require that vendors are inspected and hold International Organization for Standardization (ISO) 9001 accreditation. ISO certification indicates factories have quality management systems that meet requirements for

1. Customer focus
2. Leadership
3. Involvement of associates
4. Process approach to manufacturing
5. System approach to management
6. Continuous Improvement
7. Fact-based decision making
8. Mutually beneficial relationships with suppliers

In 2014 manufacturers in China held over 330,000 ISO 9001 certificates. That's 30 percent of all ISO certificates worldwide.[6] Yet in the same

---

[6]C. Paris. 2014. "ISO 9001 Certificates in China: How Fake Are They?" *Oxbridge Quality Resources International.* www.oxebridge.com/emma/iso-9001-certificates-in-china-how-fake-are-they/, (accessed March 15, 2017).

year Chinese goods represented 51 percent of all product safety recalls made by the U.S. Consumer Product Safety Commission (CPSC).[7] Part of the quality management problem is inspection. There are simply too many facilities exporting products to the United States compared with the number of federal inspectors. For example, in 2016 there were 23 Food and Drug (FDA) inspectors responsible for 27,000 FDA registered food suppliers. Another part of the quality management problem is the ISO certification process. In China, ISO 9001 certificates are issued by local certification bodies. These bodies should be accredited by CNAS (China National Accreditation Service). In actuality, it's not uncommon to find fake certificates, nonaccredited certifiers, or even fake certifiers.[8]

Increasingly plant requests for quotation required ISO certification. After weighing business opportunities against certification costs, the plant manager decided to hire a local ISO consulting firm to oversee certification.

During the next 5 months, consultants worked full-time at the factory. Much of their time was spent interviewing workers, creating standard operating procedures, and organizing documents.

Quality analysts were trained on using these documents and conducting internal audits. Eventually, ISO consultants conducted 3rd party audits to certify the plant.

Not long afterward, the plant received a customer complaint. The plant manager was eager to see how ISO certification would improve problem-solving. He asked the quality manager for an update.

"Did you find the root cause?"

"Yes. Some operators weren't following procedures."

"Which procedures did they miss?"

---

[7]M. Snyder and B. Carfagno. 2017. "Chinese Product Safety: A Persistent Challenge to US Importers and Regulators," *US-China Economic and Security Review Commission Staff Research Report*. www.uscc.gov/sites/default/files/Research/Chinese%20 Product%20Safety.pdf, (accessed January 18, 2019).

[8]M. Slater. 2015. "Is There a China ISO Certificate Search Website?" *China Checkup*. www.chinacheckup.com/blogs/articles/china-iso-certificate-search-website, (accessed August 18, 2018).

"It's hard to say."

"What do you mean?"

"Our procedures are more of a guide."

"That doesn't make sense. People are either doing what the procedures say or not."

"One of my responsibilities is ensuring the plant maintains its ISO certification. That means everyone is always doing what documents say."

"I know."

"Well, to reduce the risk of noncompliance our procedures are a bit general."

"How general?"

"Very general"

Another way ISO certification falls short in China is a lack of participation. As of 2002, of the approximately 20,000 ISO standards, Chinese manufacturers, research institutions, and government agencies contributed to fewer than two dozen. Why is the worldwide leader in manufacturing and ISO 9001 certification not contributing more to quality standards? With the exception of companies like Huawei, Xiaomi, Lenovo, and Haier, many Chinese manufacturers aren't designing what they make. Possibly, either buyers are providing designs or manufacturers are producing copies.

Even with designs in hand, local engineers may not fully grasp the design intent. Unlike their counterparts in the United States, Chinese engineers aren't required to pass a state-recognized Fundamentals of Engineering (FE) exam. As a result, engineering qualifications can vary widely by school and discipline.

The foreign manager needed to hire a mechanical engineer. The HR manager provided him with three resumes.

"Miss Zhang, what type of engineer is this person?"

"He's a gearbox engineer."

"So he's a mechanical engineer who specializes in gearing?"

"No. He's educated on the engineering of gearboxes."

> *"Can he work on things other than gearboxes?"*
>
> *"I don't know. You can ask him."*
>
> *"What about this person? It says he has a TV degree. Does that mean he engineers televisions?"*
>
> *"No. He received his degree through a correspondence course on TV."*

Not understanding exactly what drawings are saying doesn't stop local engineers from changing them. Changes are much more than simply translating words, symbols, projections, and units. Translated drawings can have different nominal dimensions and tolerances. They might even be made from different materials. These changes are rarely communicated to buyers. Why are local engineers changing foreign drawings? It has to do with China's system of standards.

The General Administration of Quality Supervision, Inspection and Quarantine (AQSIQ) oversees Chinese standards. Standards are defined at the enterprise (Q prefix), local (DB), professional (JB), and national (GB) levels. Enterprise standards are created and filed by companies. Local standards typically define health, safety, and hygiene requirements for particular locations. Professional standards outline rules for particular industries. Standards follow a hierarchy. Local standards supersede enterprise standards. Professional standards supersede local standards. And national standards supersede them all.[9] Chinese supply chains run smoothly when everyone is following the system of standards. For example, China's JB manuals provide rules for mechanical construction. An engineer can reference the appropriate JB design manual for the following:

1. Material selection
2. Nominal dimensions
3. Tolerances
4. And features (e.g., shoulders, radii, diameters, undercuts, tapers, keyway)

When buyers request parts made outside standards, it's likely that local materials aren't available, local equipment can't achieve tolerances,

---

[9]T in a Chinese standard indicates it's in development.

and local gauges can't measure what's being manufactured. There are also legal reasons why local engineers modify drawings to follow AQSIQ standards. Of the approximately 22,000 GB standards, 15 percent are mandatory. Anyone producing or selling products in China that fail to meet mandatory standards could be fined or could lose their business license. PRC Product Liability Law goes so far as to state that "a person who suffers personal injury or damage to property due to defects of a product may sue the manufacturer or seller of the product."[10] What counts as a product defect in China? Under China's Product Quality Law, "if there is some kind of standard a product must comply with, then there is a defect if the product does not comply with the standard."[11]

Unfortunately, specifying on POs that purchased goods and services meet applicable standards isn't enough to ensure quality. This is because Chinese standards are written from the producer's standpoint. Content centers on activities manufactures must do. Little consideration is given to what the resulting customer quality level should be. Other problems with national, provincial, industry, and enterprise standards are the excessively long development times, poor implementation, and errors.

[A machine arrived in China with U.S.-made guarding. Unfortunately, the guarding needed some modifications.]
  "Mr. Liu, have you finished altering the guards?"
  "No, it's taking a lot longer than expected."
  "Why?"
  "We broke four saw blades trying to cut a notch."
  "Is the steel too thick?"
  "We've never had any problems cutting Chinese steel of this thickness."
  "Do you want me to import some U.S. blades?"
  "No. We'd probably just end up breaking our saws."

---

[10]Lehman, Lee and Shu. 2016. "What Is the Legal Basis for Claiming Liability According to China's Product Liability Law?" www.lehmanlaw.com/resource-centre/faqs/product-liability/what-is-the-legal-basis-for-claiming-liability-according-to-chinas-product-liability-law.html, (accessed February 12, 2020).
[11]Ibid.

In 2020, the Chinese government, under advisement from AQSIQ and the Chinese Academy of Science (CAS), launched *China Standards 2035*. Under the program, the focus has shifted from writing domestic standards for local manufacturers to designing global standards for technology use worldwide. This is particularly true in the high-tech areas of cloud computing, 5G, Internet of Things, green technology and artificial intelligence. China's move into developing global standards in these areas is not without political tension. For example, Chinese telecoms giant Huawei holds most of the world's 5G patents. It, along with several dozens of its subsidiaries and affiliates, have been placed on the U.S. Dept. of Commerce's *Entity List*. The listing essentially bars U.S. firms from doing business with them. The concern, according to the Trump administration, is "over the ability of the Chinese corporation – with ties to the Chinese Communist Party and People's Liberation Army – to use its control over telecommunications infrastructure to intercept data from individuals, corporations and government."[12] Yet the only way for the United States to be part of the next generation of 5G technology is to be part of standards development that Huawei leads. For that reason the Department of Commerce has allowed U.S. firms to work with Huawei in standards setting bodies.

In response to supply chain barriers being placed around the 300 or so Chinese firms on the U.S. Entity List, the president of CAS commented: "The US' technological containment list will be our mission for scientific and technological development."[13] In addition, a noted Chinese finance professor has called for Chinese authorities to consider "exercis[ing] jurisdiction in some cases where overseas entities provide information about Chinese customers or contacts to foreign judicial bodies that cause losses. Beijing could even step in if foreign courts or governments caused damages

---

[12]J. Ball. 2019. "What's Really behind the US's Huawei Ban?" https://www. newstatesman.com/spotlight-america/cyber/2019/11/whats-really-behind-uss-huawei-ban, (accessed September 4, 2020).

[13]F. Tang. 2020. "US Technology Embargo List Gives China a Blueprint for Home-Grown Innovation over the Next Decade, Top Science Official Says," *South China Morning Post*. https://www.scmp.com/economy/china-economy/article/3101948/us-technology-embargo-list-gives-china-blueprint-home-grown, (accessed Sept. 18, 2020).

to Chinese parties."[14] Toward that end, the Ministry of Commerce announced, in 2020, the creation of an *Unreliable Entities List.* Those on the list are foreign enterprises, organizations, or individuals whose "activities harm China's national sovereignty, security, and development interests or violate internationally accepted economic and trade rules."[15] Although details have yet to be defined, possible repercussions could include fines and restrictions on investment, trade, or entry into the country.

---

[14] F. Tang. 2020. "China Urged to Flex Long-Arm Jurisdiction to Protect Its Companies from Foreign Hostility," *South China Morning Post.* https://www.scmp.com/economy/china-economy/article/3101803/china-urged-flex-long-arm-jurisdiction-protect-its-companies, (accessed September 18, 2020).

[15] *Agence-France Press.* 2020. "Amid Row with US, China Comes Out with 'Unreliable Entities List,'" https://www.ndtv.com/world-news/amid-row-with-us-china-comes-out-with-unreliable-entities-list-2297871, (accessed September 19, 2020).

CHAPTER 7

Logistics

China is the world's largest logistics market, estimated at $1.76 trillion in 2018.[1] For an economy based on supplying low-priced commodities for export, logistics in China is surprisingly expensive. For example, of the total amount spent on Chinese goods, approximately 20 percent goes into logistics. That's over twice as much as what U.S. companies spend on logistics. Half of China's logistics spend goes into transportation.

China has over 2.5 million miles of roads.[2] Village roads (as shown in Figure 7.1) account for roughly half of all Chinese roads. However, when it comes to moving freight, village roads aren't of much use. By weight, 80 percent of Chinese cargo is transported on highways.[3] Reliance on highway transport is a recent development in China. The National Trunk Highway System was launched in 1990. At that time China had about 100 miles of highway. By 2011, over 53,000 miles of highway linked every provincial capital and all Chinese cities with populations of over 200,000.[4]

---

[1]*PYMNTS.com.* 2018. "China Claims Title of World's Largest Logistics Market," www.pymnts.com/news/international/2018/china-logistics-market-transportation-costs-robotics/, (accessed February 13, 2020).

[2]*International Road and Transport Union.* 2009. "Road Transport in the Peoples Republic of China," www.iru.org/sites/default/files/2016-01/en-rt-in-china.pdf, (accessed March 19, 2018).

[3]H. Long, et al. 2005. "Investigating the Characteristics of Truck Crashes on Expressways to Develop Truck Safety Improvement Strategies in China," *The National Academies of Sciences Engineering Medicine.* https://trid.trb.org/view.aspx?id=851593, (accessed February 2, 2018).

[4]L. Guo and Z. Yang. 2017. "Evaluation of Foreign Trade Transport Accessibility for Mainland China," *Maritime Policy and Management.* https://www.researchgate.net/publication/317252235_Evaluation_of_foreign_trade_transport_accessibility_for_Mainland_China, (accessed April 15, 2019).

Figure 7.1 Typical village road

Source: Courtesy of Wu Xubiao.

China's highways are laid out in a "7 by 9 by 18" grid. Seven national roads radiate from Beijing, nine cover the country north to south, and 18 run east and west. Operations managers seeking to minimize trucking costs locate their factories and vendors within easy access of this grid.

China's highway system is not only larger than the U.S. interstate highway system but was built in half the time. Interestingly, this wasn't accomplished by following the U.S. model. The U.S. interstate highway system is funded in no small part by an 18.4¢/gallon gasoline tax and a 24.4¢/gallon diesel tax.[5] In a rare departure from the state council, the National People's Congress rejected the idea of using China's already high 95¢/gallon gasoline tax and 76¢/gallon diesel tax to pay for highway

---

[5]*US Energy Information Administration.* 2019. "How Much Tax Do We Pay on a Gallon of Gasoline and on a Gallon of Diesel Fuel?" www.eia.gov/tools/faqs/faq.php?id=10&t=10, (accessed July 6, 2019).

Figure 7.2 Map of China NTHS Expressway, 2011

Source: Adapted from "Map of China NTHS Expressway G6.png," by N. Farid, 2014, https://commons.wikimedia.org/wiki/File:Map_of_China_NTHS_Expressway_G6.png.

construction.[6] Unfortunately, vehicle purchase tax, road maintenance fees, and highway transport management fees weren't enough to cover the $240-billion price tag.[7] The Ministry of Transport (MOT) passed highway funding responsibility to the provinces. But provincial governments lacked the necessary tax revenue and borrowing power to finance construction. They entered into 25-year build–operate–transfer agreements with seven private expressway corporations. The Shenzhen Expressway, Hopewell Highway Infrastructure, and Yuexiu Transportation Infrastructure Corporation build and maintain highways in the south. Sichuan

---

[6]L. Zongwei, et al. 2017. "Overview of China's Automotive Tax Scheme: Current Situation, Potential Problems and Future Direction," *Journal of Southeast Asian Research*.   https://ibimapublishing.com/articles/JSAR/2017/790677/790677.pdf, (accessed June 7, 2019).

[7]*Road Traffic Technology*. 2012. "National Truck Highway System (NTHS)," www.roadtraffic-technology.com/projects/national-trunk-highway-system/, (accessed August 8, 2018).

Expressway handles traffic in the west. Zhejiang Expressway, Anhui Expressway, and Jiangsu Expressway (as shown in Figure 7.3) operate highways in the east.

Figure 7.3 Typical Jiangsu highway scene

Source: Courtesy of Wu Xubiao.

The primary source of revenue for expressway corporations is tolls. As of 2016, nearly 70 percent of the world's toll roads were in China.[8] Figure 7.4 is an example of a typical toll gate in China.

---

[8]B. Reja, P. Amos, and F. Hongye. 2013. "China Road Tolls Policy: Past Achievements and Future Directions," *The World Bank.* www.worldbank.org/en/news/opinion/2013/06/14/china-road-tolls-policy-past-achievements-and-future-directions, (accessed July 8, 2018).

Figure 7.4 Typical Chinese toll gate

Source: Courtesy of Wu Xubiao.

Expressways in the east and south account for most of China's traffic flow. Roads are generally in good condition because toll receipts are sufficient to maintain operations. The same can't be said for roads in the more sparsely populated central and western regions. As a whole, expressway corporations operate at a loss. In 2007 they lost $1 billion.[9] From 2010 to 2017 the situation was worse. They lost approximately $7 billion per year.[10]

Overcoming transport delays owing to poor road conditions isn't simply a matter of raising tolls. One the one hand, tolls are set by the government; on the other hand, they're already very expensive. Tolls account for roughly 20 percent of trucking costs in China. At 13¢/mile, Chinese tolls are, on average, 20 percent more expensive than U.S. highway tolls.[11] Tolls alone, however, can't explain why China's trucking costs, at $2.50 to $3 per mile, are 70 percent more expensive than those in the United

[9] *The World Bank.* 2007. "China's Expressways: Connecting People and Markets for Equitable Development," http://documents.worldbank.org/curated/en/761361468023701493/pdf /365500ESW0P09600BOX361530B00PUBLIC0.pdf, (accessed August 16, 2017).

[10] C. Yang. 2018. "Transport Ministry Tightens Toll Road Rules as Losses Spiral," *Caixin.* www.caixinglobal.com/2018-12-21/transport-ministry-tightens-toll-road-rules-as-losses-spiral-101362141.html (February 2, 2020).

[11] J. Durkay. 2013. "Comparison of Toll Rates by State and Regional Tolling Authorities," *National Conference on State Legislatures.* www.ncsl.org/documents/ transportation/NCSL_Comparison_of_Tolling_Rates_Feb_2013.pdf, (accessed July 19, 2017).

States.[12] Part of the reason is fuel cost. In February of 2020, a liter of diesel in China was 17 percent more expensive than in the United States.[13]

Another reason for the high cost of trucking in China is inefficiency. It's estimated that 40 percent of the time Chinese trucks are running empty.[14] On the surface, they're empty because much of the local, less than full truckload (LTL) business is being transported by electric bike couriers.[15] Figure 7.5 shows a typical courier delivery.

Figure 7.5 Typical electric bike courier service

Source: Courtesy of Wu Xubiao.

---

[12]T. Zongyang. 2011. "Driving Overloaded Trucks Off Highways Targeted," *China Daily*. www.chinadaily.com.cn/china/2011-03/24/content_12218917.htm, (accessed August 26, 2018).

[13]*GlobalPetrolprices.com*. 2020. "Diesel Prices Per Liter," www.globalpetrolprices.com/diesel_prices/, (accessed February 14, 2020).

[14]A. Minter. 2017. "China Transforms the Trucking Business," *Bloomberg*. www.bloomberg.com/view/articles/2017-11-30/china-transforms-the-trucking-business, (accessed March 26, 2019).

[15]I. Mir. 2013. "Logistics Revolution in China: Will Delivery Companies Deliver?" *CKGSB Knowledge*. http://knowledge.ckgsb.edu.cn/2013/06/24/china/logistics-revolution-in-china-will-delivery-companies-deliver/, (accessed September 22, 2018).

On a deeper level, China's transportation sector has a number of systemic problems. In 2016 a symposium was held in Shenzhen, China, entitled "Improving Efficiency in Chinese Trucking and Logistics." Key conclusions were as follows[16]:

- Low barriers to entry result in an oversupply of low-quality carriers.
- A proliferation of protectionist local regulations and tax codes discourage economies of scale.
- Multiple, poorly enforced regulations reduce operating efficiencies.
- Poor equipment standardization also reduces operating efficiencies.
- Modern logistics management techniques and IT systems aren't widely used.

With limited ability to electronically coordinate pickups and drops, it stands to reason that most freight in China is moved as full truckloads (FTLs). The average delivery distance is 100 miles.[17] It's estimated that when trucks have loads, 80 percent of the time they're overloaded. Figure 7.6 is a typical example of an overloaded vehicle.

Fines do little to deter overloading. For example, a truck caught exceeding height restrictions might face only a $30 to $150 fine. The standard highway toll could still apply for a truck 30 percent overloaded.[18] It could be argued that highway rules designed to improve road safety contribute to the overloading problems. Chinese trucks operate under maximum height (e.g., 13 ft.), length (e.g., 59 ft.), width (e.g., 100.4 in.), and weight restrictions. All of these limits are less than U.S. interstate highway regulations. Why not improve compliance and cost by making rules more economical to follow? Part of the problem is truck quality.

---

[16]J. Agenbroad, J. Creyts, D. Mullaney, J. Song, and Z. Wang. 2016. "Improving Efficiency in Chinese Trucking and Logistics," *Rocky Mountain Institute*. https://rmi. org/wp-content/uploads/2017/03/China_Trucking_Charrette_Report_2016.pdf, (accessed September 3, 2020)

[17]*Road Traffic Technology*. 2012. "National Truck Highway System (NTHS)," www. roadtraffic-technology.com/projects/national-trunk-highway-system/, (accessed August 8, 2018).

[18] *The World Bank*. 2007. "China's Expressways: Connecting People and Markets for Equitable Development," http://documents.worldbank.org/curated/en/761361468023701493/pdf /365500ESW0P09600BOX361530B00PUBLIC0.pdf, (accessed August 16, 2017).

Figure 7.6 Typical overloaded Chinese truck

Source: Courtesy of Wu Xubiao

The Chinese truck market is the world's largest. In 2018, 1.15 million heavy trucks (representing 50 percent of the world market) were sold.[19] Foreign builders offering the latest in safety and fuel efficiency would love to sell in this market. Unfortunately, foreign trucks are seldom, if ever, seen on Chinese roads. In 2019 two local builders (FAW Jiefang and Dongfeng Motor) split 40 percent of the market.[20] Local truck builders control the market by offering vehicles 60 to 80 percent cheaper than foreign competitors.[21]

---

[19]*360 Feed wire. 2019.* "Outlook on the Chinese Heavy Truck Industry 2019–2025 – FAW Jiefang Leads with a Market Share of 20%, Closely Followed by Dongfeng Motor with 19%," www.oilandgas360.com/outlook-on-the-chinese-heavy-truck-industry-2019-2025-faw-jiefang-leads-with-a-market-share-of-20-closely-followed-by-dongfeng-motor-with-19/, (accessed February 2, 2020).

[20]Ibid.

[21]This price gap only widens after taking into account China's 10 percent vehicle sales tax.

Inexpensive trucks are important to local buyers because half of Chinese trucking companies operate at zero to 5 percent profit margin.[22] Profits are low because the transport market is fragmented. For example, of the nine million or so trucking firms, six million are single-truck operations.[23] The top 20 carriers combined control less than 2 percent of the market.

Few companies have more to gain by improving China's transportation sector than e-commerce giant Alibaba. In 2013, Alibaba accounted for roughly 70 percent of all deliveries in China.[24] One way Alibaba is seeking to reduce delivery costs is by investing over $1 billion in a nationwide network of warehouses. Setting up warehouses to cut down on transportation cost makes sense considering the low cost of storage in China. In 2018, the average price of warehouse space in Shanghai was $0.75/ft^2 per month.[25] That's almost ten times cheaper than the average warehousing price in the United States.[26]

Standing in the way of efficiently moving freight between locations is a proliferation of local regulations. For example, a trailer weight distribution in one city (as shown in Figure 7.7) may not be permitted in a neighboring city.

---

[22]*IBIS World*. 2019. "Freight Trucking Industry in China—Market Research Report. www.ibisworld.com/industry-trends/international/china-market-research-reports/transport-storage-post/freight-trucking.html, (accessed January 22, 2020).

[23]A. Minter. 2017. "China Transforms the Trucking Business," *Bloomberg*. www.bloomberg.com/view/articles/2017-11-30/china-transforms-the-trucking-business, (accessed March 26, 2019).

[24]I. Mir. 2013. "Logistics Revolution in China: Will Delivery Companies Deliver?" *CKGSB Knowledge*. http://knowledge.ckgsb.edu.cn/2013/06/24/china/logistics-revolution-in-china-will-delivery-companies-deliver/, (accessed September 22, 2018).

[25]M. Zito. 2014. "Logistics, Warehousing and Transportation in China (Part 1)," *Dezan, Shira and Associates*. www.china-briefing.com/news/logistics-warehousing-transportation-china-part-1/, (accessed August 23, 2018).

[26]SCDigest Editorial Staff. 2018. "Supply Chain News: US Market for Warehouse Space Remains Red Hot, with Availability at Near Record Lows," *Supply Chain Digest*. www.scdigest.com/ontarget/18-07-24-1.php?cid=14473&ctype=content, (accessed June 22, 2019).

Figure 7.7 Example of Chinese truckload configuration

Source: Courtesy of Wu Xubiao.

Some cities, such as Shanghai, permit only local trucks to use high-traffic roads. Out-of-town trucks are easily identified by their license plate numbers, which, as Figure 7.8 shows, must be painted on tailgates.

Figure 7.8 Example of Chinese tailgate

Source: Courtesy of Wu Xubiao.

Traffic laws are enforced through a series of more than 170 million surveillance cameras.[27] Per Figure 7.9, CCTV cameras are seemingly everywhere.

---

[27]J. Russell. 2017. "China CCTV Surveillance Network Took Just 7 Minutes to Find BBC Reporter," *Tech Crunch*. https://techcrunch.com/2017/12/13/china-cctv-bbc-reporter/, (accessed June 23, 2018).

Figure 7.9 CCTV *cameras at every intersection*

Source: Courtesy of Wu Xubiao.

To control traffic congestion, local authorities might restrict times of day when trucks can use busy roads. It isn't unusual to see queues of tractor trailers (as those shown in Figure 7.10) waiting their allotted time to pass through cities and towns. Cameras automatically detect violations, and points are assigned. Drivers are permitted up to 12 points per calendar year.

Figure 7.10 Trucks parked along the roadside

Source: Courtesy of Wu Xubiao.

Given the high cost and inefficiencies of trucking, companies often use rail for overland shipments exceeding 200 miles. China is home to the largest railway network in the world.[28] The 50,000-plus miles of track is comparable in size to China's National Trunk Highway System. The five rail hubs and 18 intermodal yards are shown in Figure 7.11.

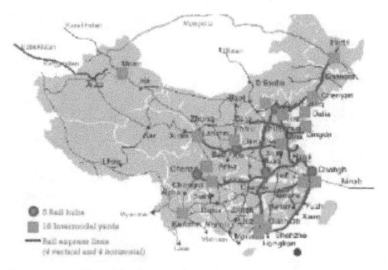

Figure 7.11 China's rail network, 2014

Source: Reprinted from "China's Transportation System and Plans for the Future," US Dept. of Transportation, 2014. Retrieved from https://international.fhwa.dot.gov/pubs/pl08020/fmic_08_03.cfm.

Like the highway system, the rail network is expanding. It's estimated that by 2030 China's rail network will stretch 93,000 miles.[29] Driving growth in the rail sector is the comparably low cost of laying tracks. The price per mile of track in China is roughly $15 million, which is at least half of the price in the United States.[30] As with highway expansion, rail expansion is being financed with debt. However, unlike highways, which

[28]F. Gronkvist. 2018. "Train Railway Freight from China: A Complete Guide," *China Importal.* www.chinaimportal.com/blog/railway-freight-china/, (accessed July 27, 2019).

[29]L. Guo and Z. Yang. 2017. "Evaluation of Foreign Trade Transport Accessibility for Mainland China," *Maritime Policy and Management.* www.researchgate.net/publication/317252235_Evaluation_of_foreign_trade_transport_accessibility_for_Mainland_China, (accessed April 15, 2019).

[30]M. Wines. 2011. "China Rail Chief's Firing Hints at Trouble," *New York Times.* www.nytimes.com/2011/02/18/world/asia/18rail.html, (accessed August 19, 2018).

rely on corporate investment, the Ministry of Rail (MOR) provided the hundreds of billions of dollars needed.

By 2011, the MOR resembled a country more than a ministry. It had its own schools, police force, and system of courts. It had also amassed close to $320 billion in debt.[31] It didn't help that the railway minister and his deputy chief engineer were accused of embezzling over $100 million. Untenable debt, widespread mismanagement, and a poor safety record resulted in the MOR being disbanded in 2013.

In its place the central government created the state-run China Railway Corporation (CR). Unlike its predecessor, CR focuses solely on railway construction and operations. Of the two activities, CR is prioritizing improvements in efficiency over simply laying more track. In terms of freight operations, CR moved about two trillion ton-miles in 2018.[32] That's roughly the same amount of rail freight moved in the United States. And as is true of the United States, Chinese rail freight accounts for roughly two-thirds of inland transport in ton-miles.[33]

A heavily reliance on rail freight makes sense considering the low cost ($0.27 to $0.32 per lb.) of using it.[34] For shipments over 435 miles, rail transport in China is 40 to 60 percent cheaper than trucking.[35] The issue is time. What takes days to move by truck might take weeks by train. Part of the problem is that Chinese freight doesn't run on dedicated lines.

[31]K. Smith. 2013. "China to Abolish Ministry of Railways?" *International Railway Journal.* www.railjournal.com/regions/asia/china-to-abolish-ministry-of-railways/, (accessed October 16, 2018).

[32]*Statista.* 2018. "Volume of Rail Freight Traffic in China from 2008 to 2018," www.statista.com/statistics/276066/volume-of-rail-freight-traffic-in-china/, (accessed November 25, 2019).

[33]P. Amos and J. Dashan. 2009. "Sustainable Development of Inland Waterway Transport in China," *The World Bank and the Ministry of Transport People's Republic of China.* http://siteresources.worldbank.org/EXTPRAL/Resources/china.pdf, (accessed May 12, 2018).

[34]F. Gronkvist. 2018. "Train Railway Freight from China: A Complete Guide," *China Importal.* www.chinaimportal.com/blog/railway-freight-china/, (accessed July 27, 2019).

[35]*The World Bank.* 2007. "China's Expressways: Connecting People and Markets for Equitable Development," http://documents.worldbank.org/curated/en/761361468023701493/pdf/365500ESW0P09600BOX361530B00PUBLIC0.pdf, (accessed August 16, 2017).

Military, passenger, coal, and food all have priority. Another source of delays is intermodal transfer. When freight cars arrive at ports, they must often be offloaded to trucks before loads are transferred to ships. The reason is that many Chinese ports were built when trucking, shipping, and rail fell under different ministries. Lack of coordination resulted in many ports (such as the one shown in Figure 7.12) being built without dockside rail access.

Figure 7.12 Example of dock with trucking but no rail access

Source: Courtesy of Wu Xubiao.

Interestingly, many of the problems companies face in moving products domestically by rail don't apply when exporting. In 2013, China exported essentially nothing by rail. By 2017, as part of the "Belt and Road" initiative, 39 rail lines linked 12 European cities with 16 Chinese cities.[36] That same year more than 3,000 freight cars made the 7,500-mile trip between China and Europe.

For operations seeking to take advantage of rail exports, it's helpful to be located along the three main rail lines shown in Figure 7.13. The northern corridor follows the Trans-Siberian Railway; the middle corridor cuts through Kazakhstan; and the southern corridor crosses Central Asia. Almost half of what's being transported along these routes is raw

---

[36]J. Webb. 2017. "The New Silk Road: China Launches Beijing-London Freight Train Route," *Forbes*. www.forbes.com/sites/jwebb/2017/01/03/the-new-silk-road-china-launches-beijing-london-freight-train-route/#4e91dfc41f13, (accessed May 23, 2019).

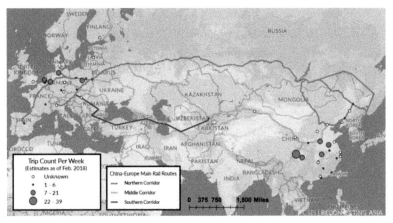

Figure 7.13 CR rail export routes

Source: Reprinted from "The Rise of China-Europe Railways," by J. Hillman, 2018, Center for Strategic and International Studies. Retrieved from www.csis.org/analysis/rise-china-europe-railways.

materials.[37] Raw materials pricing is a key problem for Chinese manufacturers. Even though China is the world's largest consumer of raw materials, closed financial markets mean global commodities prices are set by futures contracts traded in Chicago and London.

Key advantages of exporting by rail are transit time and cost. Container cars can make the trip from China to Europe in about 10 days. That's twice as fast as shipping. It's also 30 percent cheaper than shipping. The issue is that prices are heavily dependent on government subsidies. For example, from 2011 to 2016 Chinese provincial governments spent over $300 million on European routes.[38] It's estimated that government subsidies offset 60 percent of the $9,200 cost to send a railcar from China to Europe.[39]

---

[37]J. Hillman. 2018. "The Rise of China-Europe Railways," *Center for Strategic and International Studies*. www.csis.org/analysis/rise-china-europe-railways, (accessed June 12, 2019).

[38]*Mordor Intelligence*. 2018. "China-Europe Rail Freight Transport Market—Growth, Trends, and Forecast (2020–2025)," www.mordorintelligence.com/industry-reports/china-europe-rail-freight-transport-market, (accessed October 25, 2019).

[39]*Shipping Gazette.com*. 2018. "China to Scale Down Subsidies for Trains," www.vandongederoo.com/china-to-scale-down-subsidies-for-trains/, (accessed November 23, 2019).

As impressive as the growth in rail transport has been, almost 70 percent of Chinese international trade is still done by sea. When it comes to sea trade with the United States, approximately half of all containers passing through the largest U.S. ports in Los Angeles and Long Beach originate from China.

China's heavy reliance on sea trade has as much to do with what's being made as where it's being made. Traditionally, the Chinese economy has focused on the production of low-priced, high-volume commodities for exports. To cut down on transportation costs, approximately 40% of China's GDP is produced along the eastern coast, as shown in Figure 7.14.[40]

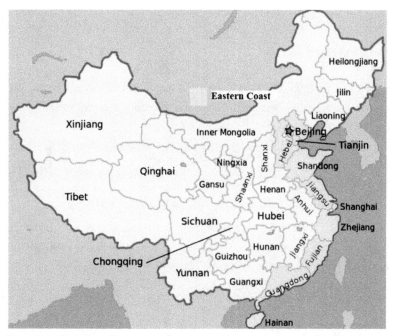

Figure 7.14 China's gross domestic product is primarily along the eastern coast, 2015

Source: Adapted by calling out east coast provinces on "Map of China en names.svg," by P. Potrowl, 2010, https://commons.wikimedia.org/wiki/File:Map_of_China_en_names.svg.

---

[40]G. Friedman and J. Shapiro. 2017. "Leading Power: A Look at Japan vs. China." *Mauldin Economic.* https://geopoliticalfutures.com/leading-power-a-look-at-japan-vs-china/, (accessed January 23, 2020).

Warehouses and factories along the coast have easy access to any one of China's top 10 shipping ports located in the cities of Dalian, Tianjin, Qingdao, Shanghai, Ningbo, Shenzhen, Guangzhou, Hong Kong, and Xiamen. Figure 7.15 shows Ningbo-Zhoushan Port, which is the world's busiest port in terms of cargo tonnage. In 2017, one billion metric tons of cargo passed through the port.[41]

Figure 7.15 Ningbo-Zhoushan Port

Source: Courtesy of Wu Xubiao.

With China exporting 50 percent more goods than the second largest exporting country, it stands to reason that seven Chinese shipping ports are among the 10 largest in the world.[42] Located at the mouth of the Yangtze River, the Port of Shanghai is the world's largest container port. In 2006, 20 million 20-foot container equivalents (TEUs) passed through Shanghai Port. Ten years later, container traffic through the port doubled.[43] To put this volume of sea containers in perspective, it's roughly three times the combined volume of the two largest U.S. container ports. Chinese exports so dominate maritime trade that two out of every three sea containers in transit globally have set sail from Chinese ports.[44]

[41]*Xinhua.* 2017. "China's Ningbo-Zhoushan Port Sees Record Throughput," www.xinhuanet.com/english/2017-12/27/c_136855637.htm, (accessed May 23, 2018).

[42]*Cargo from China Ltd.* 2019. "China Sea Freight Shipping—Everything You Need to Know," https://cargofromchina.com/sea-freight/, (accessed August 12, 2019).

[43]*The Medi Telegraph Shipping and Intermodal Transport.* 2018. "Shanghai Port Handling Capacity Breaks Record," www.themeditelegraph.com/en/transport/ports/2018/01/01/news/shanghai-port-handling-capacity-breaks-record-1.38085829?refresh_ce, (accessed November 15, 2019).

[44]*World Shipping Council.* 2014. "Trade Statistics," www.worldshipping.org/about-the-industry/global-trade/trade-statistics, (accessed May 16, 2019).

The massive size of China's shipping sector translates into low prices. For example, as of 2019, an exporter from China could expect to pay $0.85 to $1.15 per cubic foot for less than container load (LCL) shipment.[45] Full container load (FCL) rates were anywhere from $500 to $1,000 per 20 ft. container. Which shipping method is most cost effective from China? It depends. If cargo can fill at least half of a sea container, it's usually cheaper to ship FCL. If shipment weight is less than 200 kg, it's generally advisable to ship LCL. Besides weight and measure, shipping decisions depend on time of year. December through April is traditionally the slow season exporting from China. Prices are low following Christmas. From mid-January through early February, prices increase as factories are busy processing orders prior to closing for Chinese Spring Festival. May through November is the peak season leading up to the Christmas rush. During this time shippers can expect to pay higher general rates as well as peak season surcharges.

Water transport in China isn't just about ocean freight. Each year, over 100,000 river barges move more than 260 million tons of goods along Chinese waterways.[46] Barges account for nearly 10 percent of China's total inland freight by weight. Traffic is highly concentrated, with eight out of every ten barges moving goods along the Yangtze River. As the Yangtze River approaches China's eastern coast, barges can pass through the Grand Canal system. These 1,100 miles of inland waterways (as shown in Figure 7.16) date back over 2,000 years.

Canals connect five major rivers (Hai, Huai, Qiantang, Yangtze, and Yellow) across six provinces (Hebei, Shandong, Henan, Jiangsu, Anhui, and Zhejiang) and two municipalities (Beijing and Tianjin). Today, only 10 percent of these canals can be used for shipping. The northern half of the canal system is too dry for shipping. Barge transport is largely restricted to a 325-mile stretch of waterways in the south. (One such stretch is shown in Figure 7.17.)

---

[45]F. Gronkvist. 2018. "Train Railway Freight from China: A Complete Guide," *China Importal.* www.chinaimportal.com/blog/railway-freight-china/, (accessed July 27, 2019).

[46]D. Lague. 2007. "On an Ancient Canal, Grunge Gives Way to Grandeur—The Grand Canal," *New York Times.* www.nytimes.com/2007/07/24/world/asia/24canal.html, (accessed June 26, 2017).

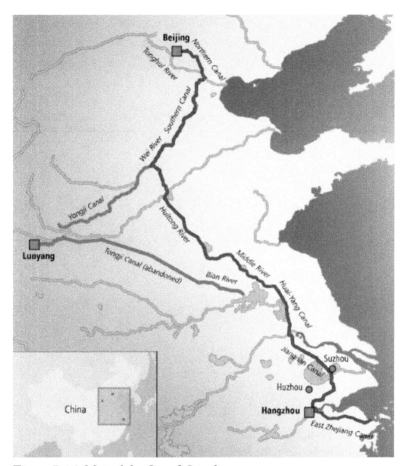

Figure 7.16 Map of the Grand Canal

Source: Reprinted from "Urban Heritage Conservation of China's Historic Water Towns and the Role of Professor Ruan Yisan: Nanxun, Tongli, and Wuzhen," by H. Porfyriou, 2019. www. researchgate .net/publication/335163611_Urban_Heritage_Conservation_of_China's_Historic_ Water_Towns_and_the_Role_of_Professor_Ruan_Yisan_Nanxun_Tongli_and_Wuzhen.

Figure 7.17 Typical barge traffic in Wuxi, China

Source: Courtesy of Wu Xubiao.

With an abundance of heavy industry and inland rail, waterway, and highway transport, the Yangtze River Economic Belt has blossomed. Today, it accounts for roughly 40 percent of China's population and 40 percent of its economic output, as shown in Figure 7.18.[47]

Figure 7.18 Yangtze River Economic Belt

Source: Reprinted from "Ecosystem services trade-offs and determinants in China's Yangtze River Economic Belt from 2000 to 2015," by X. Xu, X. Yang and G. Tan, 2018. Retrieved from www .researchgate.net/publication/324771205_Ecosystem_services_trade-offs_and_determinants_in_ China's_Yangtze_River_Economic_Belt_from_2000_to_2015.

---

[47]X. Xu, G. Yang, and Y. Tan. 2018. "Ecosystem Services Trade-Offs and Determinants in China's Yangtze River Economic Belt from 2000 to 2015," *Science of The Total Environment*. www.researchgate.net/publication/324771205_Ecosystem_ services_trade-offs_and_determinants_in_China's_Yangtze_River_Economic_Belt_ from_2000_to_2015, (accessed April 13, 2019).

Operations within the Yangtze Economic Belt typically consolidate their supply chains therein. The same can be said for operations located inside China's three largest port clusters in the Bohai Rim, Yangtze River Delta, and Pearl River Delta, as shown in Figure 7.19.

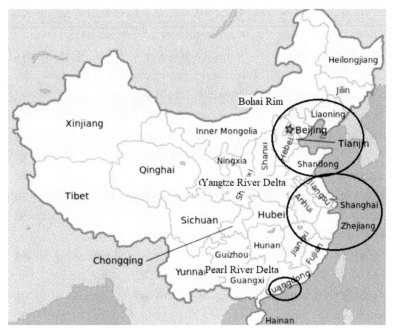

Figure 7.19 China's port clusters

Source: Added port cluster circles to "Map of China en names.svg," by P. Potrowl, 2010, https://commons.wikimedia.org/wiki/File:Map_of_China_en_names.svg.

Each of these regions is anchored by one of China's largest cities. Shanghai is located inside the Yangtze River Delta. Beijing is inside the Bohai Rim. And Guangzhou is inside the Pearl River Delta.

The Yangtze River Delta is China's richest region per capita, generating approximately 20 percent of the country's GDP and one-third of its international trade in 2016.[48] The Delta encompasses the logistics center of Shanghai, the manufacturing centers of Jiangsu and Zhejiang provinces, and the abundant natural resources of Anhui province. If anything

---

[48]M. Preen. 2018. "The Yangtze River Delta Integration Plan," *China Debriefing*. www.china-briefing.com/news/yangtze-river-delta-integration-plan/, (accessed February 21, 2020).

has been holding back development in the region, it is a lack of integration. To improve cooperation, officials from Shanghai, Zhejiang, Jiangsu, and Anhui have put together a 3-year plan (2018–20). The plan calls for investing more than $1 billion in more than a dozen collaborative projects.

What the Yangtze River Delta hub is in the south the Bohai Rim hub is in the north. It generates approximately 25 percent of the country's GDP. The Rim includes the rail and highway hubs of Beijing; the ports of Tianjin, Qingdao, and Dalian; and seven economic development zones (Shenyang Economic Development Zone, Liaoning Coastal Economic Development Zone, Zhongguancun (Beijing) Technology and Innovation Center, Caofeidian (Hebei) Circular Economy Demonstration Area, Binhai (Tianjin) New Area, Yellow River Delta Eco-Economic Zone, and Shandong Marine Economic Zone). Although provinces and municipalities in the region are highly industrialized, linkages, like those in the Yangtze River Delta, are weak. As a result, markets in the Rim are comparatively small and fragmented.

With only 5 percent of China's population and generating 10 percent of the country's GDP, the Pearl River Delta is the smallest of the country's three hubs. But foreign direct investment in excess of $1 trillion means the region accounts for 25 percent of China's exports.[49] Additional sources of revenue include Hong Kong's $4.5 trillion (HK$ 35 trillion) financial sector, Macao's $16 billion (MOP$ 128 billion) entertainment sector, Shenzhen's $100 billion (694 billion RMB) technology sector, Guangzhou's $150 billion (1.1 trillion RMB) trading sector, and the $500 billion (3.5 trillion RMB) industrial output in the manufacturing centers of Foshan and Dongguan. Coordinating capital flow in the Guangdong–Hong Kong–Macao Greater Bay Area (GBA) has been a challenge given the three different currencies in circulation. In 2020, the Central Bank of the People's Republic of China launched a series of reforms aimed at easing foreign exchange and remittance in the GBA. The

---

[49]E. Fuller. 2017. "China's Crown Jewel: The Pearl River Delta," *Forbes*. www.forbes.com/sites/edfuller/2017/10/02/chinas-crown-jewel-the-pearl-river-delta/#658af2925047, (accessed February 12, 2020).

goal, according to HSBC Bank, is to cluster talent, capital, and industry in order to drive higher value-added production and consumption.[50]

As the GBA, Pearl River Delta, Bohai Rim, and Yangtze River Delta indicate, business in China is centered in hubs. A key reason is transportation cost. With eight out of every 10 pounds of Chinese freight moving by truck, supply chains depend on road transport. Trucking being 70 percent more expensive in China than in the United States, managers set up operations within economic clusters to cut down on transportation. Each cluster is designed to have every supplier, distributor, and mode of transport necessary to support local operations. China's export focus means hubs are located either along the coast or along inland rail and waterway links connecting to the coast.

---

[50]Q. Hongbin and K. Lam. 2018. "China's Greater Bay Area: Many Cities, One Goal," *HSBC Global Research*. file:///C:/Users/seidelsonc/Downloads/greater-bay-to-drive-chinas-growth.pdf, (accessed August 12, 2020).

CHAPTER 8

Opportunities and Threats

With approximately 10 percent of China's gross domestic product (GDP) exported and 20 percent of that sent to the United States, local operations managers are counting on new logistics channels to diversify their customer base. A government effort of particular importance is the "One Belt, One Road" initiative. This government-led project seeks to connect China with[1]

- 68 countries
- 55 percent of the world's gross national product (GNP)
- 70 percent of the world's population, and
- 75 percent of known energy reserves

As shown in Figure 8.1, the "Belt" consists of highways and rail lines connecting factories in China to Russia in the north and Europe in the west. The "Road" consists of shipping lanes traversing Southeast Asia, South Asia, Africa, and Europe.

It is worth noting that Belt and Road connections are not entirely physical. The Digital Silk Road consists of fiber optics, telecommunications, artificial intelligence, cloud computing, e-commerce and mobile payment systems.

To finance all this physical and digital infrastructure, the Chinese government is lending money to foreign governments on an unprecedented scale. For example, in Africa, China is providing "more financing for

---

[1]S. Davoudi, R. Raynor, B. Reid, and D. Shaw. 2018. "Policy and Practice Spatial imaginaries: Tyrannies or Transformations?" *The Town Planning Review.* www. researchgate.net/publication/324131971_Policy_and_Practice_Spatial_imaginaries_ Tyrannies_or_transformations, (accessed August 28, 2019).

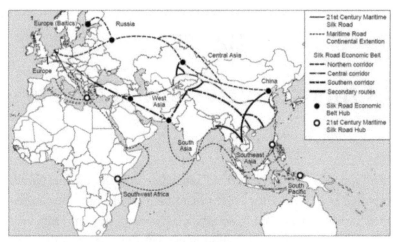

Figure 8.1 One belt and one road, 2015

Source: Courtesy of Henry Tillman at China Investment Research.

information and communications technology than all multilateral agencies and leading democracies combined."[2] Although development funding is welcome, concerns are also being raised. Officially, the Belt and Road initiative "has no publically stated KPI's, no overarching institutions, no formal membership protocols, charters, or even timelines."[3] All that's required is a nonlegally binding memorandum of understanding (MOU). When agreements are implemented, Chinese companies are typically the big winners. As of 2016, almost 90 percent of transportation infrastructure contracts have been awarded to Chinese state-run companies.[4] The result is that foreign governments have racked up massive amounts of Chinese debt in projects of questionable financing. As the 2018 U.S.–China Economic and Review Security Commission report noted, "the sovereign debt of 27 BRI countries along the road is regarded as 'junk' by

[2] *Council on Foreign Relations.* 2020. "Assessing China's Digital Silk Road Initiative," https://www.cfr.org/china-digital-silk-road/, (accessed March 3, 2021).

[3] W. Shepard. (2020). "How China is Losing Support for Its Belt and Road Initiative." *Forbes.* https://www.forbes.com/sites/wadeshepard/2020/02/28/how-beijing-is-losing-support-for-its-belt-and-road-initiative/#41a7ca821990, (accessed September 8, 2020).

[4] L. Kuo and N. Kommenda. 2018. "What Is China's Belt and Road Initiative?" *The Guardian.* www.theguardian.com/cities/ng-interactive/2018/jul/30/what-china-belt-road-initiative-silk-road-explainer, (accessed July 16, 2019).

the three main ratings agencies, while another 14 have no rating at all."[5] Djibouti, Kyrgyzstan, Laos, Maldives, Mongolia, Montenegro, Pakistan, and Tajikistan each owe more than half of their total foreign debt to China.[6] The U.S. State Department is concerned that should countries along these new trade routes find themselves unable to repay their loans, a kind of "debt book" diplomacy could ensue.[7] In this scenario, the Chinese government forgives debt in exchange for political influence and preferential access to markets. As of 2021, China has already signed debt service suspension agreements with 12 African countries.

As of 2018, the Chinese government invested about $350 billion of close to $1.4 trillion that had been committed to Belt and Road projects. By some estimates investment could ultimately surpass $4 trillion.[8] At this rate the "One Belt, One Road" initiative will be the largest overseas investment project ever launched by a single country.[9] An obvious concern for operations managers depending on these new trade routes is "Can China afford it?"

Cash flow wouldn't appear to be a problem. As of 2016, the People's Bank of China held $4 trillion in reserves. That's more money than any other central bank in the world has.[10] Furthermore, the central government's

[5]USCC. 2018. "China and the World Section 1: Belt and Road Initiative." https://www.uscc.gov/sites/default/files/2019-09/Chapter%203%20Section%201-%20Belt%20and%20Road%20Initative_0.pdf, (accessed Sept 9, 2020).

[6]L. Kuo and N. Kommenda. 2018. "What Is China's Belt and Road Initiative?" *The Guardian.* www.theguardian.com/cities/ng-interactive/2018/jul/30/what-china-belt-road-initiative-silk-road-explainer, (accessed July 16, 2019).

[7]H. Davidson. 2018. "Warning Sounded over China's 'Debtbook Diplomacy,'" *The Guardian.* www.theguardian.com/world/2018/may/15/warning-sounded-over-chinas-debtbook-diplomacy, (accessed September 12, 2019).

[8]S. Gan. 2018. "One Belt, One Road—Many Motives," *Seafarer.* www.ft.com/content/0714074a-0334-11e7-aa5b-6bb07f5c8e12, (accessed February 18, 2019).

[9]J. Meltzer. 2017. "China's One Belt One Road Initiative: A View from the United States," *The ASAN Forum.* www.brookings.edu/research/chinas-one-belt-one-road-initiative-a-view-from-the-united-states/, (accessed June 18, 2018).

[10]B. Palmer. 2012. "If Currency Manipulation Is So Great for Exports, Why Don't We Do It?" *Slate.* www.slate.com/articles/news_and_politics/explainer/2012/10/china_currency_manipulation_how_does_it_harm_the_u_s_and_what_can_we_do.html, (accessed July 16, 2019).

debt-to-GDP ratio also seems very manageable. At 43 percent it's significantly lower than the U.S. government's 103 percent ratio.[11]

However, to clearly understand Chinese government debt, all payment obligations need to be considered. For example, during the global recession, from 2008 through 2012, over one-third of China's GDP was in manufacturing, and 20 percent of everything made was exported. To protect domestic industry from the 30 percent downturn in global demand, the central government committed over $600 billion in economic stimulus spending.

The central government, however, only put up a quarter of this money. The remainder was the responsibility of local governments. Since local governments lacked the money and borrowing power to meet their obligations, they set up over 4,000 state-owned financing platforms. Within three years these state-owned enterprises (SOEs) had accumulated close to $1.5 trillion in debt. As large as local government debt is, it pales in comparison with what China's 155,000 SOEs have borrowed. Their estimated debt is close to $12 trillion.[12]

After factoring in local government and SOE borrowing, the central government's total debt obligations are approximately $30 trillion,[13] more than that of any other country in the world. It's also 300 percent of China's GDP. European countries have gone bankrupt at lower debt percentages.

What's the risk of local governments and SOEs defaulting on their loans? Since the mid-1990s, local government expenditures have exceeded revenues by an average of 20 percent.[14] SOEs haven't fared much

[11] P. Mourdoukoutas. 2016. "The Scariest Thing about China's Debt," *Forbes*. www.forbes.com/sites/panosmourdoukoutas/2016/01/18/the-most-scary-thing-about-chinas-debt/#7431252647c8, (accessed November 19, 2018).

[12] T. Durden. 2015. "Did Something Just Snap in China: Total SOE Debt Rises by $1 Trillion One Month," *Zero Hedge*. www.zerohedge.com/news/2015-11-02/did-something-just-snap-china-total-soe-debt-rises-1-trillion-one-month, (accessed September 12, 2018).

[13] J. Edwards. 2016. "How China Accumulated $28 Trillion in Debt in Such a Short Time," *Business Insider*. www.businessinsider.com/china-debt-to-gdp-statistics-2016-1?r=UK&IR=T, (accessed August 18, 2018).

[14] Y. Lu and T. Sun. 2013. "Local Government Financing Platforms in China: A Fortune or Misfortune?" *International Monetary Fund Working Paper*. www.imf.org/external/pubs/ft/wp/2013/wp13243.pdf, (accessed July 23, 2018).

better. Their return on assets have seldom exceeded 5 percent.[15] To keep high-spending local governments and low-profitability SOEs afloat, the central government has been making it easier for banks to lend. From 2010 to 2020, the People's Bank of China reduced the reserve requirement from 16 to 13 percent for large banks and 13.5 to 11 percent for small banks.[16] SOEs have been a key beneficiary of a loosened monetary policy. They accounted for 53 percent of corporate loans in 2018.[17] An unfortunate consequence of high SOE lending is that banks have accumulated close to $600 billion in nonperforming debt.[18]

It's not just the amount of nonperforming debt that's troubling but the rate of debt growth. In 2007, Chinese debt as a ratio of GDP was 121 percent. Seven years later that percentage doubled.[19] Using debt to finance growth is nothing new in China. In the decades prior to the global recession, operations managers routinely borrowed heavily, knowing that they could use increased sales to service their debt. During the recession, many companies continued with this strategy. The result was that from 2007 to 2014 Chinese corporate debt as a percentage of GDP soared 270 percent.[20]

---

[15] *The Economist*. 2014. "Fixing China Inc.," www.economist.com/news/china/21614240-reform-state-companies-back-agenda-fixing-china-inc, (accessed June 20, 2018).

[16] Y. Zhao and Y. Gao. 2020. "PBOC Sets Policy Pace for 2020 With Reserve Cut to Aid Credit," *Bloomberg*. www.bloomberg.com/news/articles/2020-01-01/china-cuts-banks-reserve-ratio-to-boost-economic-growth-in-2020, (accessed January 30, 2020).

[17] E. Tse. 2019. "Chinese SOEs Are Focused on Business, Not Politics," *Nikkei Asian Review*. https://asia.nikkei.com/Opinion/Chinese-SOEs-are-focused-on-business-not-politics, (accessed February 2, 2020).

[18] P. Sweeny, et al. 2016. "Exclusive: China to Ease Commercial Banks' Bad Debt Burden Via Equity Swaps—Sources," *Reuters*. www.reuters.com/article/us-china-banks-npls-exclusive/exclusive-china-to-ease-commercial-banks-bad-debt-burden-via-equity-swaps-sources-idUSKCN0WC0MD, (accessed August 23, 2018).

[19] J. Edwards. 2016. "How China Accumulated $28 Trillion in Debt in Such a Short Time," *Business Insider*. www.businessinsider.com/china-debt-to-gdp-statistics-2016-1?r=UK&IR=T, (accessed August 18, 2018).

[20] R. Elliot. 2016. "China's Debt is 250% of GDP and 'Could Be Fatal', Says Government Expert," *The Guardian*. www.theguardian.com/business/2016/jun/16/chinas-debt-is-250-of-gdp-and-could-be-fatal-says-government-expert, (accessed August 18, 2018).

Unfortunately, borrowing has been heaviest when economic growth is at its lowest level in the past 25 years. Today, half of all Chinese companies are paying interest at twice their earnings.[21] For example, government efforts to build a local semiconductor industry took a hit with Chinese chipmaker Tsinghua Unigroup defaulting on a $450 million bond in 2020.[22] In addition to liquidity problems, many operations in China are faced with capacity problems. Overcapacity in the iron and steel, glass, cement, aluminum, solar panel, and power generation sectors is estimated to be 30 percent.[23] If a mere 10 percent of this capacity is eliminated, close to 4 million workers would lose their jobs.[24] This would cost local governments upward of $73 billion in unemployment benefits. And banks would be forced to write off billions in bad debt.

Clearly, more money is needed to keep made-in-China functioning. The central government has responded by printing more money, which, of course, drives up inflation. How big is China's inflation problem for operations managers? The producer price index (PPI) measures what it costs manufacturers to produce. From 1995 to 2018, China's PPI increased by

---

[21]M. Bird and J. Edwards. 2015. "China's $28 Trillion Problem: 'The Dark Side of Asia's Debt,'" *Business Insider*. www.businessinsider.com/asian-debt-and-gdp-stats-2015-10?r=UK&IR=T/#china-is-the-biggest-asian-economy-and-the-biggest-problem-this-chart-shows-one-of-the-more-optimistic-growth-forecasts-for-the-next-few-years-other-economists-think-the-countrys-transformation-will-cut-growth-even-further-than-that-4, (accessed September 14, 2018).

[22]Bray, C. 2021. "China Chip Maker Tsinghua Unigroup to Default on US$450 Million Bond as Concerns Mount over Debt Levels on Mainland," *South China Morning Post*. https://www.scmp.com/business/banking-finance/article/3113357/china-chip-maker-tsinghua-unigroup-default-us450-million, (accessed March 20, 2021).

[23]S. Cheng. 2015. "Overcapacity a Time Bomb for China's Economy," *South China Morning Post*. www.scmp.com/comment/insight-opinion/article/1862024/overcapacity-time-bomb-chinas-economy, (accessed June 23, 2019).

[24]EAF Editorial Group. 2016. "Zombie Firms and China's Economic Woes," *East Asia Forum* www.eastasiaforum.org/2016/11/21/zombie-firms-and-chinas-economic-woes/, (accessed August 23, 2019).

an average of 1.30 percent annually.[25] In 2018 alone, China's PPI surged 4.55 percent.[26]

Manufacturing in China is more expensive now than ever before. Nowhere is this reflected more clearly than in wages. The ratio of wages paid per unit produced increased 250 percent from 2000 to 2010.[27]

To offset rising labor costs, operations managers are seeking to make higher value-added products. Apple products and semiconductor chips provide good examples of China's value-added problem. In 2011, manufacturers in China made eight out of every 10 iPads. Of the $250 manufacturing cost, only $10 of value was generated in China. The remaining 96 percent of value came from imported components. That same year, Foxconn manufactured all iPhone 3GS models in Shenzhen, China. Of the $600 price tag only 1 percent of the value was created in China. American companies making parts for the 3GS phones accounted for roughly 70 percent of value.[28] Eight years later, only 15 percent of China's total semiconductor consumption is supplied by China-based facilities. Moreover, foreign companies with operations in China account for almost half of chip manufacturing in China.[29]

Made in China 2025 (MIC 2025) is a government program aimed at increasing Chinese manufacturing value add. Under MIC 2025 China will transform from a manufacturing hub for clothes, shoes, and toys to IT, aerospace, medical devices, electric cars, and robots. To bring about

---

[25] *Trading Economics.* 2020. "China Producer Price Change," https://tradingeconomics.com/china/producer-prices-change, (accessed February 2, 2020).

[26] M. Zhang, L. Zhang, and R. Woo. 2018. "China's Producer Inflation Slows Again in October on Ebbing Domestic Demand," *US News.* https://money.usnews.com/investing/news/articles/2018-11-08/chinas-producer-inflation-slows-again-in-october-on-ebbing-domestic-demand, (accessed April 23, 2019).

[27] *US Dept. of Commerce.* 2017. "ACE Tool—Labor Cost," https://acetool.commerce.gov/cost-risk-topic/labor-costs, (accessed August 23, 2019).

[28] B. Chen. 2011. "Buying From China Is in Fact Buying American," *Forbes.* www.forbes.com/sites/forbesleadershipforum/2011/12/22/buying-from-china-is-in-fact-buying-american/#2258041b3d92 (November 18, 2018).

[29] D. Strub. 2019. "China's Innovation Policy and the Quest for Semiconductor Autonomy – Q&A with Dieter Ernst," American Chamber of Commerce Shanghai. https://www.amcham-shanghai.org/en/article/semiconductor-dieter-ernst, (accessed March 19, 2021).

this change, the central government has been pouring vast amounts of money into research and development (R&D). From 1991 to 2017, China's annual R&D expenditure increased 20 percent. By 2017, R&D spending reached $257 billion.[30] As impressive as that is, it's still only half of what U.S. companies spend on R&D.[31]

To close the technology gap, the central government is relying on foreign universities and foreign operations to transfer technology, talented scientists, and entrepreneurs to China. Between 2014 and 2019, Chinese SOEs, state-controlled public universities, and government-controlled nonprofits donated some $315 million to U.S. colleges.[32] At the same time, the Ministry of Science and Technology (MOST) was managing over 1,000 R&D projects worth more than $500 billion.[33] Traditionally, most of this research would have been done by the Chinese Academy of Sciences (CAS).[34] In recent years, more and more research is happening in the private sector. In 2016, 45,000 R&D organizations, or two-thirds of the total, are in private companies.[35]

Unfortunately, commercial research can be hampered by the same government agencies responsible for promoting it. For example, every

---

[30]*Xinhua*. 2018. "China's R&D Spending Sees Rapid Growth in Past Decades," www.xinhuanet.com/english/2018-09/16/c_137471687.htm, (accessed September 10, 2019).

[31]M. Boroush. 2018. "U.S. R&D Increased by $20 Billion in 2015, to $495 Billion; Estimates for 2016 Indicate a Rise to $510 Billion," *National Science Foundation*. www.nsf.gov/statistics/2018/nsf18306/, (accessed April 23, 2019).

[32]Y. Kakutani and J. Beyrer. 2021. "Organizations Linked to Chinese Military Are a Cash Cow for American Colleges," *The Washington Free Beacon*. https://freebeacon.com/campus/organizations-linked-to-chinese-military-are-a-cash-cow-for-american-colleges/, (accessed January 26, 2021).

[33]T. Kenderdine. 2017. "How Can China Afford Its Science and Technology Goals?" *Asia Scientist*. www.asianscientist.com/2017/10/features/china-science-technology-funding/, (accessed April 25, 2019).

[34]M. Springut, S. Schlaikjer, and D. Chen. 2016. "China's Program for Science and Technology Modernization: Implications for American Competitiveness," *The US-China Economic and Security Review Commission*. http://sites.utexas.edu/chinaecon/files/2015/06/USCC_Chinas-Program-for-ST.pdf, (accessed September 21, 2018).

[35]M. Springut, S. Schlaikjer, and D. Chen. 2016. "China's Program for Science and Technology Modernization: Implications for American Competitiveness," *The US-China Economic and Security Review Commission*. http://sites.utexas.edu/chinaecon/files/2015/06/USCC_Chinas-Program-for-ST.pdf, (accessed September 21, 2018).

company in China with more than 100 employees is required to have a Party group. Group leaders report directly to the central government. This gives government officials direct access to proprietary information. A company isn't likely to conduct sensitive research in China if it perceives intellectual property will be lost. This perception is reinforced by the General Office of the Central Committee of the Chinese Communist Party calling for increased Party involvement in business activities. The *Opinion on Strengthening the United Front Work of the Private Economy in the New Era* states that the Party "ought to have more influence over the management decisions of private firms, to ensure that they adhere firmly to the correct, state-determined line."[36] The *National Review* explains the logic as "capital in the hands of entrepreneurs is a political resource; it poses a threat to the implementation of centralized plans."[37]

Under the Party's MIC 2025 plan, China will be 70 percent self-sufficient in high technology by 2025.[38] The aim is to be "a manufacturing superpower that dominates [the] global market in critical high-tech industries by 2049."[39] This is a lofty plan considering that a 2021 State Council Development Research Center report places China in "the third tier in a four-tier ranking system based on key criteria including innovation, quality and effectiveness, environmental factors and global competitiveness."[40] Chinese manufacturing ambitions are very unsettling

---

[36]M. Shuman. 2021. "The Undoing of China's Economic Miracle," *The Atlantic*. https://www.theatlantic.com/international/archive/2021/01/xi-jinping-china-economy-jack-ma/617552/, (accessed March 21, 2021).

[37]M. Hochberg and L. Hochberg. 2021. "The Bill Is Coming Due for China's 'Capitalist' Experiment," *The National Review*. https://www.nationalreview.com/2021/01/the-bill-is-coming-due-for-chinas-capitalist-experiment/, (accessed March 21, 2021).

[38]J. McBride and A. Chatzky. 2019. "Is 'Made in China 2025' a Threat to Global Trade?" *Council on Foreign Relations*. www.cfr.org/backgrounder/made-china-2025-threat-global-trade, (accessed November 23, 2019).

[39]L. Laskai. 2018. "Why Does Everyone Hate Made in China 2025?" *Council on Foreign Relations*. www.cfr.org/blog/why-does-everyone-hate-made-china-2025, (accessed March 23, 2019).

[40]P. Hall. 2021. "Former Chinese Government Minister: Country Is 30 Years Away From Top-Tier Manufacturing," *Bezinga*. https://www.benzinga.com/news/21/03/20056131/former-chinese-government-minister-country-is-30-years-away-from-top-tier-manufacturing?utm_campaign=partner_feed&utm_source=SmartNews&utm_medium=partner_feed&utm_content=site, (accessed March 18, 2021)

to many countries whose only exports to China are high-technology products. The reality is that Chinese operations need to be more involved in high value-add manufacturing to solve the dual problems of rising labor costs and overcapacity. Manufacturers in China are counting on the Party's "One Belt, One Road" Party plan to address excess capacity through more exports. Critics of the plan point out that with growth rates in world trade predicted to remain below 3 percent for the foreseeable future, investing trillions of dollars in public works projects aimed at opening up cross-border trade is unlikely to pay dividends.[41] Indeed, over the last few years, investor interest in Belt and Road projects has cooled. In 2016, Chinese overseas investment grew 50 percent year on year. From 2017 through 2019, outgoing Chinese investment fell year-on-year from +23 percent to +13 percent to +0.1 percent.[42]

A dividend many Chinese operations managers are banking on is increased domestic consumption. In 2015 Chinese consumers spent $4.2 trillion.[43] That's more than French and German consumers combined. The potential for continued increases in consumption is huge. For example, as a percentage of GDP, Chinese consumers spend only half the global average. China's Development Research Centre forecasts "per capita gross domestic product will reach US$14,000 by 2024, and that China's market will be bigger than that of United States by 2025, with at least 560 million 'middle-income' consumers."[44] Yet many middle-income countries like China never achieve high-income status. To break out of

---

[41] *World Trade Organization.* 2016. "Trade Growth to Remain Subdued in 2016 as Uncertainties Weigh on Global Demand," www.wto.org/english/news_e/pres16_e/pr768_e.htm, (accessed August 23, 2018).

[42] A. Ng, A. 2019. "Why Chinese Overseas Investment Growth is Set to Slow Further," *CNBC.* https://www.cnbc.com/2019/08/21/moodys-chinese-overseas-infrastructure-investment-growth-to-slow.html, (accessed Sept. 8, 2020).

[43] Y. Kuo. 2016. "3 Great Forces Changing China's Consumer Market," *World Economic Forum.* www.weforum.org/agenda/2016/01/3-great-forces-changing-chinas-consumer-market/, (accessed September 13, 2018).

[44] H. He. 2020. "China's Inward-Facing 'Dual Circulation' Strategy Leaves Many Wondering Where Domestic Demand Will Come From," *South China Morning Post.* https://www.scmp.com/economy/china-economy/article/3100482/chinas-inward-facing-dual-circulation-strategy-leaves-many, (accessed September 9, 2020).

the "middle income trap," the Chinese government is following a three-pronged approach.

Under the "dual circulation" policy, the Chinese economy will shift away from a heavy reliance on foreign direct investment (FDI) and exports emphasizing growth through domestic companies serving local markets. Toward this end local governments are subsidizing domestic companies for their use of domestic components in key MIC 2025 business sectors. For instance, China Telecom is the largest SOE in the telecommunications sector. In 2020 it replaced foreign server ships made by Intel, Microsoft, and IBM with those made by Huawei. The hope of this effort and others like it is to create Chinese supply chains that are less dependent on imports for both R&D and manufacturing. Emphasizing domestic consumption makes sense considering China's ongoing trade disputes with the West as well as increased purchasing power at home. In 2019 China's GDP per capita exceeded 10,000 U.S. dollars for the first time in history.[45]

As the number of Chinese companies seeking to reduce their dependence on foreign trade increases, some of their trading partners are doing the same. For example, a UBS Group survey of Japanese, Korean, and Taiwanese companies that export products from China found that "85% had already relocated or intended to shift some capacity out of China."[46] To successfully realign domestic production capacity, the Chinese government, according to a former deputy head of the Development Research Centre, will need to "reduce market distortion and allocate labor, land and financial resources to higher productive areas."[47]

---

[45]*Xinhua.* 2020. "Understanding "Dual Circulation" and What It Means for World," http://en.people.cn/n3/2020/0906/c90000-9757006.html, (accessed September 11, 2020).

[46]*The Wall Street Journal.* 2020. "China's Xi speeds up inward economic shift," https://www.foxbusiness.com/business-leaders/wsj-news-exclusive-tiktok-tracked-user-data-using-tactic-banned-by-google, (accessed August 13, 2020).

[47]F. Tang. 2020. "China's New Economic Strategy to Rely on Domestic Market Is Not a Closed-Door Policy, Beijing Advisers Say," *South China Morning Post.* https://www.scmp.com/economy/china-economy/article/3096941/chinas-new-economic-strategy-rely-domestic-market-not-closed, (accessed August 13, 2020).

Ironically, the MIC 2025 government policy aimed at boosting domestic productivity could itself be described as a market distortion. In 2020 Ministry of Industry and Information Technology (MIIT) earmarked 105 projects across the country for a combined planned investment of $104 billion.[48] The idea is through state guidance and funding to transform the economy from an assembler of foreign goods to a developer of new technologies. To ensure there is sufficient local talent to develop and support these new technologies, central and provincial governments are pouring money into education. For example, in the manufacturing hub of Shenzhen city upward of $25 billion is being invested to build 20 new universities and colleges by 2025.[49] State-directed transformation of the economy isn't without risk. In 2010, the central government invested heavily in domestic solar energy. By 2017 China was the worldwide leader in manufacturing solar modules. An unfortunate consequence of subsidies driving so many companies into solar power was massive overcapacity, followed by a worldwide drop in price and, ultimately, a string of bankruptcies.

Whether motivated by government subsidies or by servicing the growing middle class, more and more Chinese companies are manufacturing high-tech products. Most of these new factories aren't in the small towns and villages that house two out of every three Chinese operations today. Factories of the future require higher skilled workers and more developed infrastructure, both of which are more easily found near large cities. Indeed, by 2025, it's predicted that upward of 70 percent of Chinese people will live in cities.[50] Urban workers don't come cheap. They earn, on

---

[48] F. Tang. 2020. "China to Pump Hundreds of Billions of Yuan into Key Industry Projects, with 'No Need to Cover Up Its Ambitions,'" *South China Morning Post.* https://www.scmp.com/economy/china-economy/article/3101218/china-pump-hundreds-billions-yuan-key-industry-projects-no, (accessed Sept 12, 2020).

[49] H. He. 2021. "China's Hi-tech Hub Guangdong Sees Higher Education Investments Boom in Bid to Rival Silicon Valley with Home-Grown Talent," *South China Morning Post.* https://www.scmp.com/economy/china-economy/article/3118886/chinas-hi-tech-hub-sees-higher-education-investments-boom-bid, (accessed January 25, 2021).

[50] I. Johnson. 2014. "China Releases Plan to Incorporate Farmers into Cities," *New York Times.* www.nytimes.com/2014/03/18/world/asia/china-releases-plan-to-integrate-farmers-in-cities.html, (accessed March 23, 2018).

average, twice as much as those working in towns and villages. High-tech manufacturing will need to cover the high cost of their urban workforce.[51] For example, in 2018, average salaries in Beijing were just under $1,500 per month. Before operations managers consider how to justify the high cost of an urban workforce, it's important to remember that government planners face many challenges urbanizing such a vast number of people. China has more than 500 million subsistence farmers. Turning them into factory workers will involve moving hundreds of millions of people into newly constructed towns and cities.[52] Many of these transplanted farmers will lack the necessary skills to compete for urban jobs. They'll also face a much higher cost of living. At the same times, cities will have to handle the influx of people on a massive scale. One estimate puts the cost of building new roads, hospitals, schools, and community centers at $600 billion.[53]

With debt already exceeding equity by 300 percent, how is the Chinese government going to pay for the largest urbanization project the world has ever seen while, at the same time, footing the bills for transforming into a "dual circulation" economy and the largest Belt and Road infrastructure project undertaken by a single country? The Ministry of Finance (MOF) is counting on public private partnerships (PPPs).

The World Bank describes PPPs as long-term contracts between private parties and government agencies to provide public assets or services.[54] In China's case, the government parties are the Ministry of Commerce (MOC) and National Development and Reform Commission (NDRC). They're in charge of steering local governments into PPPs. As of 2014

---

[51]J. Xue and W. Gao. 2012. "How Large Is the Urban-Rural Income Gap in China?" *Research Center for International Economics.* http://faculty.washington.edu/karyiu/confer/sea12/papers/SC12-110%20Xue_Guo.pdf, (accessed August 23, 2018).

[52]J. Collier. 2014. "China's Urban Sprawl," *The World of Chinese.* www.theworldofchinese.com/2014/03/chinas-urban-sprawl/, (accessed May 23, 2018).

[53]I. Johnson. 2013. "China's Great Uprooting—Moving 250 Million Into Cities," *The New York Times.* www.nytimes.com/2013/06/16/world/asia/chinas-great-uprooting-moving-250-million-into-cities.html, (accessed June 23, 2018).

[54]H. Thieriot and C. Dominguez. 2015. "Public-Private Partnerships in China," *International Institute for Sustainable Development.* www.iisd.org/sites/default/files/publications/public-private-partnerships-china.pdf, (accessed February 23, 2018).

there were 1,043 PPP projects worth a total of $0.5 trillion.[55] Two years later, the number of PPPs skyrocketed 1,300 percent. PPPs are now worth about 25 percent of China's GDP.[56]

There are, however, issues with PPP financing. According to the World Bank, private parties in PPPs bear a significant amount of risk and responsibility. In China's case, this isn't happening. Local governments require a lot of money. In order to attract investment on such a massive scale, they've been promising very high rates of return. In some cases they've even offered to compensate investors for losses. An obvious problem with absorbing so much risk is that local governments may not have the money to back up promises. Lack of private sector faith in government-led projects can also be seen at the national level. SOEs and government policy banks have provided more than 95 percent of Belt and Road funding.

Clearly, China's development model is changing. Onerous investment rules are being replaced with new financing mechanisms. Debt is at an all-time high. Efforts are underway to abolish laws that treat foreign and domestic companies differently. And more and more Chinese companies are among the world's largest, technologically advanced operations. For example, in 2017, Chinese Internet giant Tencent was valued at $300 billion, making it one of the 10 most valuable companies in the world.[57] In 2015, the first "unmanned factory" was opened in China. Six hundred assembly line workers were replaced with 60 robots.[58] In

[55]*Deloitte.* 2014. "What is Public-Private Partnerships?" www2.deloitte.com/cn/en/pages/real-estate/articles/what-is-public-private-partnerships.html, (accessed March 23, 2018).

[56]X. Wang and F. Wang. 2017. "China Steps Up Scrutiny of Public-Private Partnerships," *Caixin.* www.caixinglobal.com/2017-11-13/china-steps-up-scrutiny-of-public-private-partnerships-101169970.html, (accessed March 23, 2018).

[57]D. Weinswig. 2017. "Tencent's New Strategy," *Forbes.* www.forbes.com/sites/deborahweinswig/2017/05/05/tencents-new-strategy/#7a151ef014b8, (accessed January 30, 2020).

[58]V. Yu. 2019. "You're Wrong: Chinese Factories Don't Only Make Poor Quality Products," *Manufacturing and QC Blog.* www.intouch-quality.com/blog/youre-wrong-chinese-factories-dont-only-make-poor-quality-products, (accessed January 2, 2020).

2020, Alibaba unveiled its first smart factory, named Xunxi. With its entire workflow recorded digitally, Xunxi is one of 10 factories recognized by the World Economic Forum as transforming manufacturing.

Clearly, the future of manufacturing in China is changing. Yet the more some things change, the more other things remain the same. China is still a highly regulated, manufacturing-based economy. Rising labor cost and low efficiency continue to be problems. And many FIEs remain focused on making labor-intensive, low-priced commodities for export out of fear that technology transferred or developed in China will be lost or stolen.

Given the threats to and opportunities for manufacturing in China, successful operations managers are the ones who can find balance. On the one hand, they profitably give consumers what they want, when they want it, at an acceptable price and quality level. On the other hand, they're constantly adapting manufacturing methods and strategies to match China's continually changing business environment.

About the Author

Dr. Craig Seidelson has spent over 20 years in manufacturing, during which time he worked 16 years in China, building and managing factories. He is presently a reviewer for the *International Journal of Operations Research and Information Systems*.

As professor of operations and supply chain management at the University of Indianapolis, he teaches logistics, quality management, and manufacturing at the undergraduate and postgraduate levels. He also teaches a course on manufacturing in China. Dr. Seidelson routinely publishes and consults on these topics. He also presents his research at conferences around the world.

Through his work as vice president of the board at the America China Society of Indiana, he brings together U.S. and Chinese businesses. His contributions in China were recognized with an honorary professorship at Changsha University of Science and Technology.

Index

OTHER TITLES IN OUR SUPPLY AND OPERATIONS MANAGEMENT COLLECTION

Joy M. Field, Boston College, *Editor*

- *How Efficiency Changes the Game: Developing Lean Operations for Competitive Advantage* by Ray Hodge
- *Supply Chain Planning: Practical Frameworks for Superior Performance* by Matthew J. Liberatore
- *Sustainable Quality* by Joseph Diele
- *The Cost: A Business Novel to Help Companies Increase Revenues and Profits* by Chris Domanski
- *Why Quality is Important and How It Applies in Diverse Business and Social Environments, Volume I* by Paul Hayes
- *Why Quality is Important and How It Applies in Diverse Business and Social Environments, Volume II* by Paul Hayes
- *The Barn Door is Open: Frameworks and Tools for Success and Fulfillment in the Workplace* by Serge Alfonse
- *Operations Management in China, First Edition by* Dr. Craig Seidelson
- *The Practical Guide to Transforming Your Company by* Dr. Daniel L. Plung
- *Logistics Management: An Analytics-Based Approach* by Tan Miller
- *Moving the Chains: An Operational Solution for Embracing Complexity in the Digital Age* by Domenico LePore
- *Leading and Managing Strategic Suppliers* by Richard Moxham
- *The New Age Urban Transportation Systems, Volume I* by Sundaravalli Narayanaswami
- *The New Age Urban Transportation Systems, Volume II* by Sundaravalli Narayanaswami

Concise and Applied Business Books

The Collection listed above is one of 30 business subject collections that Business Expert Press has grown to make BEP a premiere publisher of print and digital books. Our concise and applied books are for…

- Professionals and Practitioners
- Faculty who adopt our books for courses
- Librarians who know that BEP's Digital Libraries are a unique way to offer students ebooks to download, not restricted with any digital rights management
- Executive Training Course Leaders
- Business Seminar Organizers

Business Expert Press books are for anyone who needs to dig deeper on business ideas, goals, and solutions to everyday problems. Whether one print book, one ebook, or buying a digital library of 110 ebooks, we remain the affordable and smart way to be business smart. For more information, please visit **www.businessexpertpress.com**, or contact **sales@businessexpertpress.com**.

Printed in the USA
CPSIA information can be obtained
at www.ICGtesting.com
JSHW011510301223
54504JS00007B/120